Working in Accountancy

Working in Accountancy: A guide to qualifying and starting a successful career in accountancy

This first edition published in 2011 by Trotman Publishing, a division of Crimson Publishing Ltd., Westminster House, Kew Road, Richmond, Surrey TW9 2ND

© Trotman Publishing 2011

Author Sherridan Hughes

The right of Sherridan Hughes to be identified as the author of this work has been asserted by her in accordance with the Copyright, Designs and Patents Act, 1988.

British Library Cataloguing in Publication Data
A catalogue record for this book is available from the British Library

ISBN 978 1 84455 423 2

Typeset by IDSUK (DataConnection) Ltd
Printed and bound in the UK by Ashford Colour Press, Gosport, Hants

Working in Accountancy

A guide to qualifying and starting a successful career in accountancy

Sherridan Hughes

Contents

Contents

Useful accounting terms

You may be familiar with a few of these abbreviations already, or they might be completely new to you. In this book we will usually expand the initialisations to give the terms in full; however, you can always turn back to this page to refresh your memory.

AAT: Association of Accounting Technicians

ACA: Designation of qualified member of ICAEW or ICAI

ACCA: Association of Chartered Certified Accountants, or designation of member thereof

ACMA: Designation of qualified member of CIMA

AIA: Association of International Accountants

AIM: Alternative Investment Market

ATT: Association of Taxation Technicians

Big Four: Four largest accountancy firms: Deloitte, KPMG, PwC and Ernst & Young

blue chip: Nationally recognised, well-established, quality, financially secure and stable firm, able to maintain performance in all economic climates

BTEC HND: Higher National Diploma awarded by BTEC

CA: Designation of qualified member of ICAS

CAT: Certified Accounting Technician

CCAB: Consultative Committee of Accounting Bodies

CEO: Chief executive officer

CFO: Chief financial officer

CIMA: Chartered Institute of Management Accountants

CIOT: Chartered Institute of Taxation

CIPFA: Chartered Institute of Public Finance and Accountancy

CPD: Continuing professional development

CSR: Corporate social responsibility

CTA: Chartered Tax Adviser

DEFRA: Department for Environment, Food and Rural Affairs

ERP: Enterprise resource planning

FMCG: Fast-moving consumer goods

FTSE 100: Hundred largest UK companies listed on London Stock Exchange and in *Financial Times* indices

GAAP: Generally accepted auditing practice/principles

ICAEW: Institute of Chartered Accountants in England and Wales

ICAI: Institute of Chartered Accountants in Ireland

ICAS: Institute of Chartered Accountants in Scotland

IFRS: International Financial Reporting Standards

I&TR: Information and technology risk

NVQ: National Vocational Qualification

PER: Practical Experience Requirement

Useful accounting terms

POB: Professional Oversight Board

SMEs: Small and medium-sized enterprises

SVQ: Scottish Vocational Qualification

UCAS: Universities and Colleges Admissions Service

Introduction

The stereotype of the boring, serious accountant, tapping away on a calculator and poring over spreadsheets in the backroom, is often far from the reality. Yes, when you start, there may be some routine number-crunching, but how much depends on the sector, specialism and role in which you find yourself. Accountancy is varied, influential, prestigious and lucrative, and it is viewed as an excellent springboard into senior decision-making roles, as indeed evidenced by the fierce competition for training places. It also involves a great deal more contact with people than you might expect – which is one of the reasons team-working and interpersonal skills are emphasised in recruitment.

Never mind Napoleon's 'nation of shopkeepers': the British seem to be a nation of accountants. Every business tends to have at least one accountant, and there may be more professionally qualified accountants in the UK than the rest of the EU put together. The Financial Reporting Council's Professional Oversight Board's publication 'Key Facts and Trends in the Accountancy Profession' (June 2011) finds that in the UK and the Republic of Ireland, the seven main accountancy bodies currently support, qualify and represent more than 304,000 members and in excess of 172,000 students.

Accountants are found in all sectors – financial services, manufacturing, commerce and the not-for-profit sector – performing in many roles, from highly technical and analytical work, to production of financial reports, to financial control, to more strategic planning and management. They can work in internal roles, or externally, in professional, advisory services. Accountancy can provide a solid foundation for broader commercial, operational and systems roles as well. A large proportion of board members are accountancy-qualified and it is clearly a qualification that confers credibility and marketability, and boosts career prospects. Indeed, a sound understanding of finance is often viewed as imperative for a director.

Accountancy is open to graduates of any discipline, but the selection criteria and professional qualifications are rigorous. You will need to ensure that you are thoroughly prepared, with a strong academic record, impressive CV and good understanding of the various qualifications, roles and specialisms. Of course, you do not have to be a graduate, and there are school-leaver and on-the-job programmes, which lead to a professional qualification as well.

Introduction

The aim of this book is to provide information, tips and starting points for those considering, or already committed to, entering the field of accountancy. It will help the reader to make informed choices between the main professional bodies, the qualifications they offer, and associated costs, and the careers to which they may lead. It will provide tips for the reader to help in finding training places and to ensure strong applications in what is a highly competitive arena (last year, Grant Thornton had 8,500 applications for its 230 trainee places). We will identify some alternative entry points and routes for those without the required UCAS points, or perhaps with minimal educational qualifications.

So why do so many people choose accountancy? What exactly is attracting them?

A survey of graduates in 2010 identified the aspects of the profession that influenced people to enter it (see table 1).

TABLE 1: The UK Graduate Survey 2010 AGR/*The Times*

Professional qualifications	33%
Long-term career prospects	32%
Quality of training and development	31%
Job availability	25%
Starting salaries	25%
Relevance to degree subject	25%
Interesting work	24%
Intellectually demanding	22%
Job security	19%
Work-life balance	14%

Having a 'solid professional qualification' seems to be as important and valued as ever, and people still view this as a safe ticket to a stable, successful career. It is noteworthy that only 24% of respondents mentioned finding the subject interesting (they may come to do so when they are working in the field, but it was not what attracted them in the first place), but high starting salaries and security, which featured to a roughly equivalent extent, will no doubt be an even greater attraction in the future given the increasing cost of higher education.

The relevance of accountancy to the subject of their degree was a motivator for 25% of graduates, and people who are good with numbers often gravitate naturally towards it. However, recruiters recognise the need for balance and variety in teams, and they realise that graduates from disciplines other than business, finance, science and engineering have valuable complementary skills and qualities – they do not want a company of clones. What attracts you to accountancy? Why do you think it would suit you? Perhaps you are unsure that it would? This book should help you to make a more informed decision.

In the final chapter, we will see how the profession is optimistic about its future in this ever changing world, and accountancy is clearly likely to remain the career of choice for many of our most talented and ambitious graduates.

Throughout the book, we have also included case studies from accountants who have been in the same position you are in now, to give you some insider knowledge of what it's like to train as an accountant, and also profiles from training providers and relevant accountancy organisations.

1

Overview of the accounting profession

What is accountancy?

"You have to know accounting. It's the language of practical business life. It was a very useful thing to deliver to civilization. I've heard it came to civilization through Venice which of course was once the great commercial power in the Mediterranean. However, double entry bookkeeping was a hell of an invention."

Charlie Munger

Accountancy is an ancient profession, with the earliest records found in Mesopotamia dating back over 7,000 years. As business evolved, so did the sophistication of accounting records and financial statements. In the first instance records were purely for the business person's own interest, such as simple records of crop and herd growth, but by the fourteenth century in northern Italy, double entry bookkeeping emerged, recording investments from multiple parties for wider and more varied stakeholders.

This necessitated the introduction of accounting systems and records. For internal audiences this meant management accounting – the basis for commercial and operational decision-making, while for external interested parties and shareholders financial accounting developed, providing more structured reports for banks, economists, investors and creditors. Later, controls were introduced in the form of external regulation and neutral attestation, or auditing.

When we manage our personal finances – saving and checking receipts against our bank statements and logging incomings and outgoings – we are, in effect, acting as an accountant. If we do not study and balance earnings against outgoings, we might have an inaccurate picture of our financial situation and overspend and overstretch ourselves, until pulled up by the bank.

Accountancy involves recording, collating, summarising, interpreting, and communicating financial information. It is the 'language of business', conveying details about a company's broader economic resources and viability, and pinpointing which parts of the company are more and less profitable. Accounting technologies are pivotal to business practices in keeping track of performance. One set of accountants prepares the accounts, then (in larger concerns) a second set, the internal auditors, checks them to ensure accuracy and compliance with legislation. A third troupe, the external auditors, provides an independent rubber stamp of accuracy, or of 'true and fair' representation. Of course, should things go wrong, there could even be a fourth contingent to save or liquidate the business. Business problems tend to be diagnosed in accountancy terms and thus remedies are proposed in terms of accounting solutions and technologies, arguably fuelling the demand for yet more accountants!

Accountants need to be very commercially aware, with quantitative, logical and analytical ability, and training in finance, law and tax. Accountants in-house may prepare profit and loss statements and provide data for annual reports. They may control and oversee payroll, billing and invoicing, or advise on tax, pension schemes, contracts and budgets. They may further contribute ideas about operational efficiency or strategic direction and investments. Accountants are trained to employ structured accounting techniques to pinpoint high margin or loss-making activities. These techniques are vital to the firm's successful operation.

External accountants act more like consultants and inspectors, policing to ensure that nothing fraudulent or irregular is happening and suggesting how the firm could make or save more money or pay less tax, while remaining within the framework of the law.

Where do accountants work?

The answer is anywhere and everywhere. There is certainly no typical employer, but the three main sectors may be categorised as follows:

1. Public Practice (independent accountancy firms offering professional services)

2. industry and commerce (businesses)

3. non-commercial organisations (public sector and not-for-profit bodies).

Public Practice

There are about 5,000 professional or Public Practice firms in the UK. These are predominantly accountancy firms, which offer audit and professional services and consultancy services, to fee-paying, public limited and private company clients. Chartered Accountants (ACA) and also chartered certified (ACCA) accountants work in these, and in smaller numbers, in particular professional specialisms and divisions, so may chartered management (CIMA) accountants and chartered public finance (CIPFA) accountants. Their accountancy service offerings can be largely divided into audit, tax, and advisory. 'Advisory' comprises everything not related to audit and tax, such as mergers and acquisitions, corporate finance, performance improvement, risk and so on.

The Big Four

The largest of these Public Practice firms, namely PwC, Deloitte, Ernst & Young and KPMG, are commonly referred to collectively as the 'Big Four'. These handle the vast majority of audits for publicly traded companies and large private companies. They are actually each a network of global firms, which share a common name, brand and quality and which are coordinated by their central body (which does not itself practise accountancy or own or control the firm). Many of the founders of these firms were early presidents of the ICAEW: William Welch Deloitte, Arthur Cooper, Sir William Peat, and Frederick Whinney. There were originally eight major players, but a series of mergers and amalgamations have gradually caused these firms to evolve into four huge entities.

How the 'Big Eight' became the 'Big Four'

The Big Four evolved from an original 'Big Eight'. Until 1987, these were: Arthur Andersen; Arthur Young & Co.; Coopers & Lybrand; Ernst & Whinney — having been until 1979 Ernst & Ernst in the US and Whinney Murray in the UK; Deloitte Haskins & Sells — until 1978, Haskins & Sells in the US and Deloitte & Co. in the UK; and Peat Marwick Mitchell — later Peat Marwick, and then KPMG; Price Waterhouse; and Touche Ross.

Further mergers created the 'Big Six' (1989–1998: although in reality somewhat more complicated, Ernst & Whinney merged with Arthur Young to form Ernst & Young; and Deloitte, Haskins & Sells merged with Touche Ross to form Deloitte & Touche), and then further amalgamations whittled it down again to the 'Big Five' (1998–2001: Price Waterhouse merged with Coopers & Lybrand to form PricewaterhouseCoopers).

Involvement in the 2001 Enron scandal resulted in the (since overturned) conviction and demise of Arthur Andersen, leaving only the Big Four.

These four firms alone employ approximately 64% (nearly 47,000) of the accountants working in Public Practice, leaving just 34% (nearly 27,000) to work in middle-tier or smaller high street practices, or as sole traders. There are some other very large firms, but it is hard for them to grow significantly, because all but one of the FTSE 100 companies, and 240 companies of the FTSE 250, are said to be audited by Big Four firms. There is often debate and controversy about the power and monopoly of such audit oligopolists.

Often top graduates aspire to working in one of these firms, perhaps because they are so competitive and prestigious, not to mention the generous remuneration (in London), and golden hellos/settlement packages (typically £1,000 to £1,500, and perhaps even £1million at senior levels). Training and qualification with a Big Four practice does hold kudos and may even be seen as a requirement in a job's person specification. However, you should not simply take the path well trodden without forethought. Stop to consider whether these environments would really suit you best or whether you may in fact prefer, or be better suited to, the cosier ethos and more balanced lifestyle of a smaller or middle-tier practice (see chapter 3 for more on this).

TABLE 2: The Big Four Public Practice firms, UK, 2011

Firm	UK revenues (2011)	Employees	Headquarters
1. PwC (PricewaterhouseCoopers)	£2,331m	UK partners 845 (female 118) 16,000 employees 2,670 trainees 40 UK offices	US
2. Deloitte Touche Tohmatsu	£1,953m	UK partners 681 (female 95) 11,400 employees 2,020 trainees 21 UK offices	UK
3. Ernst & Young	£1,356m	UK partners 533 (female 91) 8,400 employees 1,328 trainees 21 UK offices	UK
4. KPMG	£1,602m	UK partners 545 (female 76) 10,500 employees 2,088 trainees 22 UK offices	NL

PricewaterhouseCoopers

The PricewaterhouseCoopers (PwC; www.pwc.com) global professional services network is the largest revenue-generating practice in the UK and employs over 161,000 people across 154 different countries. In 2011, it was pipped by Deloitte as the largest global firm in the accounting industry in terms of annual revenue. PwC has 40 offices nationally, and about 40% of the FTSE 100 companies are audited by PwC.

The name stems from the merger of Price Waterhouse and Coopers & Lybrand in 1998, but rebranding in 2010 gave birth to PwC.

For the last seven years, PwC has been voted first in *The Times* Top 100 Graduate Employers and it climbed to fourth in *The Sunday Times* Best Big Companies listing in 2010, the highest ranking among professional services firms that year. PwC has additionally received technical accolades, including Top Professional Services Adviser of 2010 at the Insurance Day awards, Employee Benefits Consultant of the Year and Actuarial Adviser of the Year at the Financial Times Pension & Investment

Provider Awards, and Employee Benefits Consultancy of the Year and Sponsor Covenant Adviser of the Year at the Professional Pensions Awards. Also named Upper Mid Market M&A Adviser of the Year in the Acquisitions Monthly awards, the company is said to 'dominate in audit and restructuring'.

Service lines are separated into:

- assurance

- tax advisory

- advisory (performance improvement, strategy, corporate finance, recovery and so on)

and broad industry specialisms of:

- consumer and industrial products and service

- financial services

- technology, communications and entertainment

- infrastructure, government and utilities.

It is an interesting fact that, since 1934, PwC has acted as tabulator and certifier of votes for the Academy Awards, but, unfortunately, the company may also be remembered for its slap on the wrist from the House of Lords in 2011, for not identifying the flaws and risks in the business model of Northern Rock, the bank that was nationalised in 2008 after suffering a run in the credit crisis.

In 2010, PwC's community contribution came to £8.1million. Supported by its Matched Giving Programme and Volunteering Awards Scheme, 4,865 of its UK staff gave 42,480 hours to support community activities (1,187 employees also volunteered in their own time).

PwC is committed to improving its sustainability: in the UK last year, it succeeded in lowering CO_2 emissions by 4.2%. PwC has taken a pivotal role in shaping the sustainability debate, and was heavily involved in COP 15 at Copenhagen. The organisation leads the Climate and Development Knowledge Network, and has written up a thorough 'Appetite for Change' survey, and 'Low Carbon Economy Index' report. Discerning graduates are increasingly asking about such issues at interview, and PwC may therefore be particularly appealing if you are interested in 'green' issues.

'Word on the street' suggests that PwC is rather bureaucratic and corporate; the promotion structure affords little flexibility until you have been there more than four years. Salary may be rather more affected by the department's success, and visibility by the importance of your clients; in other words, it may lack meritocracy. However, the workforce is very diverse with good opportunities for women, and it is said to have a strong training scheme and a supportive culture. The dress code may also be rather more relaxed (smart casual rather than suits at times), but PwC employees are sometimes described as arrogant or elitist. Perhaps this is because the company aims to employ the best. Either way, if you are competitive and believe you are the best, this may, of course, suit you.

Deloitte

Deloitte (www.deloitte.com) is a member of the global professional services group Deloitte Touche Tohmatsu (DTTL). DTTL is a private company established in the UK and limited by guarantee. In 2010, it just nudged ahead of PwC to become the largest private professional services network in the world based on aggregate member firm revenues and headcount (rather than UK revenues). Deloitte has 170,000 staff across 150 countries, with plans to recruit an additional 50,000. It has 21 offices nationally in the UK, employing 11,400 people and recruiting over 1,400 graduates and undergraduates each year.

Deloitte's service line offerings are divided into:

- audit and enterprise risk

- consulting

- financial advisory (e.g. corporate finance, insolvency and forensics)

- tax

- other, for example international financial reporting.

Deloitte has performed well in recent industry awards. In 2011 the company received 12 awards at the seventh annual International Tax Review (ITR) European Tax Awards. In 2010 it won nine awards, including Asia Indirect Tax Firm of the Year.

Additionally, Deloitte was listed in *The Sunday Times* 25 Best Big Companies to Work for 2011 and voted second in *The Times* Top 100 Graduate Employers 2010 for the fifth consecutive year. Deloitte is committed to diversity, as reflected in its Global Retention and Advancement of Women Council, the Global Diversity and Inclusion Community of Practice, and its recognition of International Women's Day. In 2010, Deloitte was recognised as having the best flexible working and family-friendly policies, and excellent flexible career opportunities, in the Workingmums.co.uk top employer awards. At the Race for Opportunity awards, Deloitte's Employability Initiative won the prize for Collaboration and Partnership. One to consider if you are planning to be a working parent, then.

Deloitte21 is a Deloitte network-wide global initiative to help disadvantaged young people acquire the education and skills required to thrive in the twenty-first-century economy. The firm is also committed to sustainability and people issues. Deloitte (UK) is also a sponsor of the 2012 Olympics and the only of the Big Four firms to have a specialist sports business group.

What do people in the industry say? Deloitte is said to have a friendly, practical, 'work hard, play hard', team-spirited culture, with strong two-way communication encouraged and practised. It professes to be committed to diversity, but may not actually be as diverse as other firms. Arrogance is again a criticism levelled. There are said to be early promotion opportunities but training often needs to be self-initiated. Perks are good (interest-free loans, moving expenses, private gym), with dinner and taxis provided when you work late. Deloitte has the reputation of being the most innovative of the Big Four, so if you like to think creatively, this could perhaps be the firm for you.

Don't mention the Haringey Council Refresh Project, a local government IT project whose estimated costs of £9million spiralled to £24.6million, despite Deloitte working on both sides of the fence, as the consultants and the auditors!

Ernst & Young

Ernst & Young (www.ey.com) is one of the longest established of the Big Four. Ernst & Young LLP is the UK member of Ernst & Young Global. It employs more than 141,000 people across 700 offices, providing professional services in 140 countries, and has a very impressive revenue and client list. In the UK, Ernst employs 8,400 staff in 21 offices.

The company's service lines are categorised as:

- assurance

- advisory (actuarial, IT risk and assurance risk, and performance improvement)

- taxation

- transaction advisory.

In 2011, Ernst & Young was three times a winner at the Scottish Accountancy Awards, and won two Management Consultancies Association Awards (for Public Sector Outsourcing and Change Management). In 2010 Ernst was recognised for its commitment to CSR, landing three Business in the Community Awards for Excellence, as well as technical awards for tax and pensions.

Ernst has been committed for 15 years to sponsoring arts, gallery and museum exhibitions, as well as the well-known Entrepreneurs of the Year Awards and educational programmes for children.

Through its Profitunity scheme, students from 10 universities raised £68,000 for the Prince's Trust, of which Ernst & Young is a patron. Ernst & Young is said to have a strong reputation for corporate finance. It is also committed to CSR, people and diversity issues, with generous maternity and paternity provisions.

Ernst would no doubt prefer to forget its involvement in the Anglo Irish Bank hidden loans controversy, in which they failed to detect during audit some large, irregular loans to the bank's chairman. In 2009 the bank was criticised by politicians, resulting in a 99% drop in share price, and in turn necessitating a bailout by the Irish government. The CEO at the Central Bank of Ireland commented that 'a lay person would expect that issues of this nature and this magnitude would have been picked up'. It cost the Irish people about £4,800 per head.

People in the profession say the culture of Ernst & Young is particularly friendly and liberal. New open-plan offices (even partners do not have their own office and the 'hot desk' policy means that you may change desk daily) promote a relaxed, supportive and open climate. There is a roughly even male/female mix and flexible working is possible, but salaries may be slightly lower than in the other three firms. Ernst is said to have quite a flat hierarchy and it favours the ICAS qualification which crams early on to build technical competence quickly. If you want to reach middle management rapidly, then Ernst could be for you. Equally, globalisation is a reality at Ernst, and it is said that many choose the firm for its strong international opportunities.

KPMG

KPMG (www.kpmgcareers.co.uk) – the result of five mergers of European firms – employs over 135,000 people in 46 countries, (10,500 in the UK), and has a network of 144 offices globally (22 in the UK). KPMG works with 71% of the FTSE 350 companies, and audits 24% of the FTSE 100 firms.

KPMG service lines are broken into:

- audit (the firm is particularly strong in this area)

- tax (business, personal and Asian)

- advisory (transaction, corporate finance, risk, forensic, IT, restructuring and performance, etc.)

- other (China).

KPMG also prides itself on its awards for people and technical excellence. It is consistently in the top 10 of *The Sunday Times* Best Big Companies to Work For; in 2009 the company received a special lifetime achievement award in view of this, and came ninth in 2011 (the highest ranking of the Big Four). In 2011, KPMG was named 'World's Best Outsourcing Advisers'.

KPMG is the only member of the Big Four firms to have a full-time dedicated Professional Qualification Training (PQT) team. This consists of 17 people (most of whom have studied the qualifications themselves) who provide help and support to graduates throughout their training.

In recent years, KPMG have put a greater focus on the environment and demonstrate this by allowing all their people half a day of firm time to volunteer in their local community each month. Over the past year alone, 39% of their people contributed 41,200 hours to communities through volunteering, and the firm's total community investment rose to £11.1million. They've also won several 'Best Giving Something Back' awards too.

Remote working is actively embraced, and the contributions of employees are recognised and rewarded via highly competitive salaries, plus a bonus scheme which reflects individual performance and allows everyone to share in KPMG's success.

Profile: KPMG

At KPMG, the people make the place. And what's that place like, exactly? In short, it's one where everyone feels valued, and hard work is recognised and rewarded.

It's also a place that's growing. Since a number of European firms merged to form KPMG Europe LLP, they have become the largest fully integrated accountancy firm in Europe, offering audit, tax and consultancy services to everyone from oil companies to music gurus.

But it's not just what KPMG does that's important. It's the way that they do it. The values don't just live on a wall. They're a way of life, underpinning the way KPMG works with clients and with each other.

So what can graduates look forward to at KPMG? Exposure to clients from day one. Working on challenging projects. And if they're studying for a professional qualification, there's a fantastic support network that includes a mentor and generous study leave.

Despite the focus on qualifications, it's not all work and no play. Whether it's joining societies and sports teams or enjoying volunteering days, free lunches and secondment opportunities, KPMG is a fantastic place for graduates to start developing their technical and personal skills.

KPMG would like to hear from graduates with at least a 2:1 degree in any discipline. And, once they've applied, they can expect a response on the next working day.

To stand out from the crowd, graduates need to apply early. Head straight for www.kpmg.co.uk/accountancy

Case study

Sophie Grierson is a Public Sector Auditor with KPMG.
She studied at Cambridge University and now works at Canary Wharf.

"I joined KPMG in October 2009 following an internship with the firm during my second year at university. Before my internship I was uncertain whether I wanted to study to become an accountant or pursue another direction, but my experience as an intern gave me a frank overview of life at KPMG and I went back to university knowing unequivocally that I wanted to complete the ACA qualification.

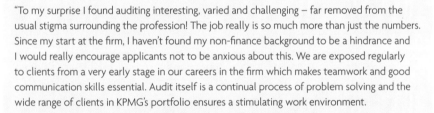

"During the application process and my internship I was immediately struck by the enthusiasm, approachability and helpfulness of the people from KPMG. This period helped shape my decision and confirmed that I had made the right choice of career with the right firm.

"To my surprise I found auditing interesting, varied and challenging – far removed from the usual stigma surrounding the profession! The job really is so much more than just the numbers. Since my start at the firm, I haven't found my non-finance background to be a hindrance and I would really encourage applicants not to be anxious about this. We are exposed regularly to clients from a very early stage in our careers in the firm which makes teamwork and good communication skills essential. Audit itself is a continual process of problem solving and the wide range of clients in KPMG's portfolio ensures a stimulating work environment.

"My day-to-day role involves working closely with a range of clients from hospitals to local government. The nature of our work means that we really get to the nuts and bolts of how the country provides public services and help to support the delivery of improved services. The public sector is a dynamic and evolving sector, particularly given the current economic climate, which makes it extremely exciting to work in.

"Our department is sociable, supportive and extremely friendly, which has had an immeasurably positive impact on my time with the firm. We have department-wide socials every couple of months, which provides an enjoyable work-life balance.

"My advice to those applying would be to think hard about which sector they would be best suited for and to be proactive in finding out more about the industry. Our clients are what make the job both challenging and interesting, so it is important to take the time to consider what sector you might thrive within.

"What has impressed me most about life at KPMG is the supportive nature of the firm and the inspiring people within it. KPMG is a place where you can reach your goals and surpass them with the support of peers and colleagues. This is an important consideration for any job and what I feel sets KPMG apart from their competitors. I am confident that this is an area within which KPMG shall continue to excel."

Does the size of Public Practice firm make any difference?

Graduate training in Public Practice for chartered accountancy qualifications (ACA) involves securing a mandatory three-year salaried training contract with one of over 2,200 providers in the UK and internationally, accredited by the Institute of Chartered Accountants in England and Wales (ICAEW) or Scottish/Irish equivalents (ICAS and ICAI). The vast majority of Chartered Accountants train in Public Practice.

Depending on your academic qualifications, on which qualification you want to study, and on which specialism or service division you want to work in, Chartered Certified Accountants (ACCA), Chartered Management Accountants (CIMA) and Chartered Public Finance Accountants (CIPFA) may also secure such training contracts with these large 'audit' firms, or with one of many other smaller professional practices, but these are not a mandatory requirement for qualification – obviously, not everyone can work for one of the Big Four firms. With training and experience in industry, accountants may also move into Public Practice post-qualification.

The standard of training should be consistent whether you go for a large, medium or small employer, because the quality demanded for ICAEW approval (or ACCA or the other organisations) is very high. Thus, the choice of training employer will be largely a matter of your own preference, and, of course, the employer's requirements in terms of academic credentials (higher qualified individuals tend to study for ACA) and experience.

Large international firms

In large firms, you are likely to be assigned to a specialist area, such as audit (the main career destination for most trainees), corporate finance or tax, whereas a smaller firm might offer broader, across-the-board experience, although these can be specialised as well, (in forensic accounting, for instance). Larger firms obviously have more openings – the Big Four have many thousands of trainees – but they are largely situated in bigger cities and towns. You are not, therefore, restricted to working in London, or even the UK. Clients tend to be FTSE 100 firms and multinationals.

Starting salaries may be higher, but hours will be long, even well into the small hours, on occasion. Some firms can have a tough 'up or out' policy, and it is common to be expected to leave should you fail the professional examinations (repeated retakes would not be acceptable), or should you not progress appropriately and it become evident that you are not seen as partner material. However, it can be exciting and challenging to join and work with a cohort of young, intelligent, ambitious and thrusting accountancy trainees who are on the fast track together. Table 3 shows how many trainees of each major professional body are currently studying with Big Four firms.

TABLE 3: Numbers of trainees in Big Four, 2011

	Total trainees	ICAEW	ICAS	ACCA	CIMA	CIPFA
PwC	2,670	2,330	200	140	n/a	n/a
Deloitte	2,020	1,515	109	101	295	0
KPMG	2,088	1,336	547	169	n/a	36
Ernst & Young	1,328	145	843	247	93	0

Training and career pathways tend to be structured. It may take longer to secure a senior role in a larger firm, but then there may be fewer management tiers and it should be possible to make executive director within nine to 12 years and senior executive partner within 10 to 15 years (the same as with smaller organisations).

Medium-sized firms

These tend to be firms with a network of offices and regional practices, and varying numbers of employees and partners, but the client list may be no less impressive than for large firms and may include independent, international and 'big name' businesses. In medium-sized practices, you may have greater responsibility more quickly and better team spirit, and it may be relatively easier to move up the ranks.

The Big Four firms do have the resources and clients to cream off the most talented graduates, and even those training in smaller practices can eventually gravitate to the bigger practices post-qualification, because of the higher salaries and greater opportunities. However, the reverse can also at times occur, when disillusionment sets in at a bigger firm and people seek a different cultural setting or specialism, or perhaps a more niche clientele.

Medium-sized practices should be large enough to cope with a diverse client range, and small enough to still be friendly and to afford scope for individuality. There may be less choice in starting point – all graduates may start in audit, for example – but progress should be quite meritocratic. With somewhat smaller clients, the audit may take as little as one or two weeks rather than six to nine months, as with the biggest clients of larger firms, and you may be able to do most of the work yourself rather than just taking responsibility for a small part.

As with large firms, training is likely to include internal support from the training division, internal technical training and external professional training from an accredited provider, who should liaise closely with the company to ensure that trainees are on track for examinations, and who should advise the firm should additional assistance be warranted. Regular feedback may be provided by your personal mentor, and you may have six-monthly reviews with your counselling partner regarding IPD (the required ICAEW log of practical experience).

Small firms

Smaller firms tend to offer a more personal approach to individual, partnership and small business clients. Some people find it particularly rewarding to advise and work more closely with freelancers, self-employed professionals, business owners and start-ups, and the work is likely to cover all aspects of accountancy. In general practice, you usually work in a small team on accounts preparation, end of year audit and tax matters, and you are quickly familiarised with the key issues for small business success.

In smaller firms there is likely to be a more personal touch and accountants will work closely with a wide range of people and businesses to advise, manage tax and financial affairs, control and reduce costs, improve systems and generate growth and wealth. They may be more able to recognise individual differences and to assure a client that their needs are being fully understood and professionally and accurately addressed. Smaller firms still need to invest in training, systems and software to keep fees competitive while providing quality services.

Clients may include high street estate agents, restaurateurs, travel agents, and all manner of retailers, as well as local builders and property developers, recruitment, media and information service companies, and many professionals, including career consultants, pharmacists, physiotherapists, doctors and surveyors. Smaller firms may pride themselves on being honest, active, accessible members of their clients' teams and may have a high client retention rate.

You are likely to enjoy a more balanced lifestyle in a small high street practice, with little if any travel. You are less likely to be confined to working in a bigger town. You are also likely to gain experience across the board, widening your expertise more rapidly, although there are some small specialised practices as well. Of course, you may even aspire to opening your own small practice in the future.

Industry and commerce

Here, you would work internally in the finance department of a commercial company, in industries including retail, telecommunications, transport, FMCG, banking and manufacturing. You can move into an in-house role post-qualification in Public Practice, or you might train internally (where the favoured qualification is often CIMA/ACCA, although there are increasingly greater ACA training opportunities – the different qualifications are discussed in the following chapter). All large companies and most small and medium-sized firms will fund study and provide leave for trainee accountants to pursue professional qualifications. Obviously, studying on the job will provide you with valuable experience and industry insight.

Accountants in-house budget for and control monies coming into and going out of the firm, in addition to considering operational efficiency, or strategic direction, funding and investments. They might work in a generalist role in a smaller firm, or in a more specialised reporting, analysis, control, taxation or corporate finance capacity in a larger organisation.

In-house you obviously work with the same colleagues and internal clients, which may suit you better should you not enjoy constantly regrouping and working with different teams and clients. With national and global concerns there may still be some travel involved. You are perhaps also better placed to see the long-term results of your interventions.

Internal accountants may not adhere to the traditional image of an accountant. You may be working with a broader range of people, trying to ensure that non-finance colleagues understand the numbers and the implications thereof. You can choose to work for a company where you have some interest in the subject matter, whether manufacturing or a service industry. Graduate programmes often involve rotational six-month placements, affording variety and broader commercial experience and insight. As a trainee in manufacturing, you could be thrown straight in, with immediate responsibility for two product lines and two teams reporting directly to you – quite a baptism of fire! From there you might, for example, move to the marketing team as a commercial analyst, evaluating product changes, costings, seasonal promotions and even which products to put in a selection box or gift pack.

A typical day might involve checking correspondence, liaising, meeting and taking conference calls with departmental managers to discuss project budgets, figures and strategy, and preparing financial data for presentations. With time you should have increasing responsibility and ownership of projects and results, liaising with senior decision makers across the company, and perhaps even external parties, subcontractors and stakeholders. It can be fun to identify, locate and tap the person with the necessary information in a larger company, and to be party to high-level commercial strategy and decisions. Internally, you are immediately putting theory into practice, consolidating learning.

Again, it can be hard to work and study simultaneously, but, as stated, study days and exam leave are usually offered by larger firms. It helps to be driven, adaptable and strong in time management.

Public sector and charities

> "It's easy to make a buck. It's a lot tougher to make a difference."
>
> Tom Brokaw

This includes public sector (local and central government), not-for-profit (charities and NGOs), NHS and educational concerns. The public sector was not historically a big trainer of Chartered Accountants (the pertinent qualification has traditionally been CIPFA) but there are increasing opportunities for this. Many accountants of all qualifications transfer into the not-for-profit sector post-qualification or later in their career, when seeking greater work-life balance or when their personal values become more social and altruistic, and less materially focused (not that pay in this sector is as poor as many may think, or efficiency any less important).

In the public sector the work involves managing income, for example rent and council tax, and making best use of public funds, advising and working with managers to maximise and improve service provisions in accordance with budgets and communities' needs. There are roles in the public sector similar to those in practice: for example, audit and tax specialists. Again, there are accountants in professional practice who, while not employed by the public sector, have 'public sector' specialisms – they may deal solely with public sector clients, for instance – so in a way, you can have your feet in both camps at once.

Obviously, this would suit you better if you are more politically and socially focused. While there is not likely to be as much travel in local government, you may need to attend some meetings locally and nationally with partner organisations, funders and contemporaries in other organisations. There may equally be job opportunities abroad with the EU, or in NGO and development organisations.

Interestingly, accountants have moved increasingly towards the public and not-for-profit sectors. It is unclear whether this is because we have entered an era of 'do-gooding', philosophy and ethics, or because people are seeking greater security and balance in insecure economic times (not that the public sector has recently been safe from the cuts). Fortunately, it has always been considered beneficial to bring commercial thinking to the non-commercial sector.

What are the main roles in accountancy?

"The pen is mightier than the sword, but no match for the accountant!"

Jonathan Glancey

In professional practice, business, industry and the non-commercial sectors discussed above, there is a great variety of potential roles, ranging from analytical policing and advisory, to control, to strategic functions. These days, there seems to be much more movement between both sectors and roles; indeed, one of the joys of accountancy is the variety and the scope for constant change and challenge it affords.

Financial accounting

Financial accountants work in Public Practice and internally in companies. They produce the summary financial statements and reports required predominantly by external stakeholders and agencies – stockholders, stockbrokers, banks, suppliers, government agencies and media groups – but obviously these might be of value internally, too. Information is taken from accounting records and published at least annually for the benefit of interested parties. This also involves forecasting and developing projections, and perhaps revising accounting and reporting policies.

Your key responsibilities might include period-end reporting, potentially within tight deadlines, management of the preliminary and year-end audits in collaboration with the firm's auditors, management and review of budgets, implementation of controls processes, and mentoring of colleagues and associates.

Month-end

- Preparation of all month-end journals (prepayments, depreciation, provisions and accruals)

- Monthly payroll reconciliation and query resolution, bank reconciliations and currency account conversions

- Completion of monthly financial close

- Reconciliation and sign-off of all balance sheet control accounts to month-end deadlines

- Production of financial and management reports, with commentary

- Production of actual/budget comparisons, investigating variances as necessary

Compliance

- Filing within statutory deadlines all tax and fiscal requirements

- Responsibility for local and international VAT (or equivalent) records and returns

Audit

- Producing accounts with backed-up audit file

- Managing all local audits

- Ensuring complete, accurate local fiscal reporting within deadlines

- Providing support and documentation for tax advisers for annual returns and compliance

Additional

- Monitoring local cashflows

- Providing group cover as required

- Working effectively with, and supporting, all members of the organisation, including perhaps staff management.

Financial accounting is quite similar to the role of an information officer, but it does afford scope for personal judgements and estimates – in line with 'generally accepted accounting principles' (GAAP) and the 'convention of objectivity' in accounting – and as with taxation, you can look at things in different ways. However, you tend to be dealing with historical rather than timely data, and the work is quite retrospective (although new technology is improving currency of data).

Unlike in management accountancy and financial analysis, you would not typically be considering non-monetary factors such as business competition, the impact of new technical innovations, loyalty and competence of staff or even currency changes, and you would be working with aggregates rather than digging into the detail of, say, which products may be performing better. It is more about reporting than changing things (management accountants, financial controllers and directors have more scope to shape how things are done), which could be frustrating if you are more proactive and forward-looking in your style.

> *"A bank is a place which will lend you money if you can prove you don't need it."*
>
> *Bob Hope*

Profile: Chartered Institute of Payroll Professionals

cipp

the **chartered institute** of **payroll professionals**

leading the profession

The Chartered Institute of Payroll Professionals (CIPP) is the only membership body for payroll professionals in the UK and currently has in excess of 5,000 members enjoying a range of benefits.

The advice and support offered by the CIPP are ideal for accountants who wish to offer payroll services to their clients and the CIPP is the leading provider of professional payroll qualifications in the UK.

In addition, the CIPP has a pensions faculty delivering qualifications and membership services to those responsible for public sector pensions.

The mission statement of the CIPP is: **Leading payroll and pension professionals through education, membership and recognition.**

Education

The CIPP is the leading provider of qualifications, training and consultancy for payroll professionals in the UK. Our payroll qualifications programme was originally formed in 1991 and is updated each year. The latest developments to our payroll programme include the introduction in September 2008 of a foundation degree in Payroll Management, accredited by Worcester University, and a new BA in Applied Business and Management, aimed at encouraging strategic thinking in payroll, which was launched in July 2011. The payroll qualifications programme goes all the way to MSc in Business and Payroll Management and aims to get more payroll staff in the boardroom.

As well as our industry recognised qualifications, the CIPP boasts a wide range of payroll training courses to increase professional knowledge in specific areas such as statutory payments, termination payments, overpayment recovery and changes to legislation. We have also recently relaunched our Pensions for Payroll Professionals training course.

Membership

The CIPP is the only professional body for people working in payroll in the UK, and has a separate pensions faculty to represent public sector pensions professionals. The CIPP has an excellent position within government to represent our members' views. This also means we can keep you abreast of changes in legislation through a number of communications channels including:

- News On Line – a weekly e-newsletter
- *PayrollProfessional* magazine issued ten months a year
- Advisory Service – a helpline you can call on during office hours
- members-only sections of the website to network and discuss topical issues.

Recognition

The CIPP is working hard to increase recognition of the importance of payroll in business, and we achieved chartered status for the profession in 2010. The policy team are now representing members' views at over 60 government consultation forums — which highlights that HMRC and other government departments recognise the important part that payroll plays in the UK economy.

Find out more about the CIPP by visiting www.cipp.org.uk, emailing info@cipp.org.uk or calling 0121 712 1000 and quoting reference WIA2011.

Case study

Interview with a CIPP graduate: Dries De Coster MCIPPdip, graduated 2009

What is your career background?
"I came from a sales background in IT and joined Employer Services Ltd (esl) without any prior payroll or HR knowledge. Whilst at esl, I achieved my payroll qualification. I currently work in a sales and account management capacity for Accero Cyborg (July 2010)."

What are your reasons for obtaining a payroll qualification?
"Coming into the industry without any knowledge of payroll meant I had a very steep learning curve and little time to obtain the knowledge I needed.

"Enrolling in the CIPP Payroll Diploma (now the Foundation Degree in Payroll Management) course meant that I was able to obtain the payroll knowledge I previously lacked. Completing the qualification has given me the confidence and credibility to have in-depth payroll conversations with clients and prospects."

What do you enjoy the most about your studies?
"The continual journey of discovery into the payroll subject matter. The more I learn, the better equipped I am to do my job."

What are the main challenges?
"The honest answer is juggling your work time and family commitments with the study time required. It is by no means impossible to do this but careful planning and dedication are required. Personally, I found my fellow students to be a great source of encouragement in helping me with this."

What do you think are the benefits of getting a payroll qualification?
"Having the qualification raises your profile both within the organisation you work for as well as to potential employers but, more importantly, it gives you the knowhow and consequent confidence in your day-to-day payroll dealings."

What advice would you give to someone who is considering doing a payroll qualification?

"Don't think about it, just do it! When the hard work is done, there is nothing like the satisfaction of receiving your qualification."

In what ways have your studies brought about a change in your perception of your role and that of payroll?

"Most people, be it through personal or professional circumstances, 'fall into' the payroll profession. Rarely have I met anyone who sets out to work within the payroll industry.

"Because of this, most of us don't regard our own role as highly as we should. Studying for a payroll qualification gives both the job role, and the payroll industry as a whole, the professional outlook it deserves."

Auditing and assurance

Perhaps the majority of Public Practice ACA trainees 'do their time' in auditing at the start of their career, but there are also internal audit roles. The reality of auditing is that it is technical and lacking in variety, and it often involves long hours and substantial travel (up to 90% of the time when not studying, although one trainee had been lucky enough to never have more than a two-hour commute). Audit involves retrospective, independent tests and checks, usually as a team on the clients' premises, assessing the accuracy, honesty and risk of an organisation's financial situation. Do company and bank records match? Do employees really exist? How much is stock really worth? Most accounting firms will have developed a set audit methodology based on generally accepted auditing standards (GAAS).

Auditing can be seen as policing, but it has a consultancy or 'value-add' element as well, in that recommendations may be made regarding how business processes, procedures, systems and controls might be improved, and perhaps 'selling' the client additional services. Auditors ensure that monies which go in and come out of a company are recorded and processed accurately. Auditing is often what people think of when they think of accountancy, but it is noteworthy that only 30% of qualified accountants work in this field.

Your key responsibilities might include:

- developing and maintaining positive relationships with clients and colleagues (indeed, you may need great diplomacy in situations where there is disagreement between the client and the auditor)

- collating data, and scrutinising and analysing spreadsheets

- checking company accounts

- testing financial control systems, according to set models, tools and techniques

- identifying and assessing levels of financial risk within organisations

- ensuring that financial reports and records are accurate and reliable (referring to original entries and reading between the lines)

- ensuring that assets are safeguarded

- identifying if and where processes are flawed or failing, and advising on changes to be made

- preparing reports, commentaries and financial statements

- liaising with managers and presenting findings and recommendations

- using in-depth knowledge of accounting legislation to ensure compliance with procedures, policies, legislation and regulations

- undertaking reviews of wages.

By its nature, audit cannot be all that exciting – you are mostly just checking invoices, accounts, data and controls – but there are some people who love it. Some people say it is varied due to the clients, while also, at the most junior level, perhaps being quite administrative – arranging couriers, photocopying and clearing up. You do need to be patient and accept that you will need to learn, and work your way up from the bottom. In large structured firms, you may have several set tasks in the first year and then several set tasks the following year, so you will simply be duplicating a process with different clients. You may feel out of your depth initially and then once you understand how it works, it may become tedious. However, asking for something more challenging may be all that is required should you begin to feel jaded!

The ethos will differ depending on with whom, and for whom, you are working. You may have a micro-managing boss, or one who is hands-off. Some managers will let you go when your work is done; others will make you stay until everyone is finished. You may have a fun team to work with, but these will often be people you have never previously met, and you do have to adapt readily to new people and environments. Obviously, this can be a good learning experience and you might consciously study your managers' techniques and body language (good and bad). You may make friends and then never see them again (not a bad thing if you did not gel, of course). Some clients resent your presence, are uncooperative and make life difficult – which is perhaps why people skills are so often emphasised by recruiters; you may need to charm them into helping and providing necessary information! January to March tends to be the busiest period.

The amount of study will vary according to the organisation. You may do 9.00am until 4.00pm in college, which can be intense, with up to an hour's homework and perhaps the same length day at weekends to keep up. It may be quite difficult to grasp until applied in practice, and everyone would admit that working and studying is hard. Some firms have 18 weeks in college in the first year to cover all 12 'knowledge' modules. There may be five days' study leave for each week of college. In the first three months, one trainee had spent a month at college, three weeks on training courses and five weeks in a hotel, but had enjoyed the variety. Whatever the task, be patient, stick to the job in hand and do it with confidence and enthusiasm.

While people skills are emphasised, the reality is that you may spend about 10 hours per day looking at a computer screen – some take an hour for lunch, others work straight through – but hours will vary slightly, depending on the job. Some trainees claim to have never had to stay beyond 5.45pm, but remember there could be substantial travel time on top of this. You might start with just a laptop and then start to acquire various secure USB drives and wireless internet cards. The first two hours of the day may well be spent trying to access the network! If staying away – you can be out of the office for months at a time and posted anywhere nationally – then you will be housed in a hotel locally, but given that clients may be situated outside the city, a car may be an advantage.

On the positive side, it is a secure, well-paid job which can lead on to more exciting and challenging work in the future. You are working with the brightest and most ambitious people and can build lasting friendships with your fellow trainees, and some people really do actually enjoy audit for its own sake. It is also a solid grounding in accountancy which may expose you to many different companies and industries.

Profile: National Audit Office

Challenge

The work of the National Audit Office covers the whole of central government spending. It is complex, varied and challenging. Our financial audit work involves auditing 470 accounts a year, representing hundreds of billions of pounds. We also publish around 60 high-profile Value for Money reports a year, which often hit the headlines. It's a great time to join us with all the attention being paid to improving the delivery of public services and achieving good value for the taxpayer.

Impact

Our Financial Audit and Value for Money work helps save the country millions of pounds a year (more than £1 billion in 2010) and helps to improve public services. We have a great reputation for professionalism, rigour and judgement.

Success

The NAO's pass rates for the ICAEW exams are consistently around 10% above the national average. We provide generous study leave, relevant work experience which allows you to put what you study into practice and an excellent system of support.

Careers

You will benefit from a range of ongoing career development opportunities designed to equip you with the skills you need to develop into a potential leader of tomorrow. Our very best people advance rapidly and a great many of the people who qualify with us choose to stay with the NAO.

Life

We take the welfare and well-being of our staff seriously, with a range of policies to support you and to ensure that you have a life outside of work as well as inside. We are committed to diversity.

So, where can I find out more and apply?

Visit big-on.org.uk to find out everything you need to know about the campaign and to complete the online application process.

Key facts

What we do: The National Audit Office scrutinises government spending on behalf of Parliament

Number of employees: 880

The scheme: Professional training scheme leading to an accountancy qualification (ICAEW)

Starting salary: London £27,160, Newcastle £21,608 + benefits

Number of graduate vacancies: 70 in London, 10 in Newcastle

Minimum requirements: A minimum of a 2.1 in any degree discipline and at least 300 UCAS points

Application deadline: 31 January 2012

Contact: HR team – 020 7798 7227, hrservicedesk@nao.gsi.gov.uk

Case study

Rachel Savage is an Audit Specialist at PwC

Why did you choose audit?

I was lucky enough to get a summer placement with PwC and from that was offered a job. What attracted me in the first place was the variety of the role – you can look after large listed clients and family-run businesses at the same time and learn a lot and very different things from both. I also believe it offers an unrivalled grounding in and understanding of businesses, which, coming from a very unrelated degree, I needed. I was also attracted to the chance to work overseas and since starting I have worked on jobs in New York, Chicago and Oregon along with most of the UK.

What do you do on a typical day?

I don't think there is a typical day! I tend to get into work early and then it depends on my clients. I spend as much of my time with my clients and my teams as possible, so that means I can be in quite a few different places each day. A core part of my role is coaching the team through the work and then reviewing it. I also spend a lot of time in meetings with the clients and the partners to ensure we are on track.

I also look after one of our social groups in the department so spend time ensuring we are meeting all our internal measures and planning for the next night out, so a bit different from the 'day job'!

How is that different now from when you first started?

Wow – very different. When you first start you spend blocks of time at each of your clients and are on site all day working through the detail. When you get to senior manager (my level), you have to run between your clients making sure your teams understand what they are doing and ensuring everything is going to plan. I spend a lot more time reviewing work than doing it now and discussing the key aspects of our audit with the client teams.

What are the best and worst bits?

The best bits are definitely when I get to help clients through problems they are facing or in some way help develop the teams I am working with.

The worst bits – probably timesheets and trying to remember where I spend my time each week!

What skills do you need?

You need to be hard-working, able to adapt and apply your skills to different situations and enjoy variety. I think most importantly, you also need to be able to get on with people. Whenever I say I am an accountant most people think you have to be good with numbers, I think being an auditor means you have to be good with people. You need to be able to talk and build relationships with your clients and coach your teams through the work.

Any other tips?

Like in most jobs, I think you also need to be able to have fun and bring your own personality and opinion to this role.

Taxation

"The hardest thing to understand in the world is the income tax."

Albert Einstein

Tax has regulatory compliance, corporate governance and more proactive planning aspects. Annual tax returns need to be completed and submitted, but careful and detailed analysis and problem-solving can also enable tax specialists to make suggestions for financial restructuring, to ensure that client companies or individuals pay the minimum legally possible (often saving them substantial sums) and understand the implications of legal decisions and contracts.

Tax is quite 'verbal', being as much about law as about numbers, and the work may have more of a routine, in that you have an ongoing relationship with clients and you primarily work from your own office. You can work internally with a large firm or in Public Practice, advising on corporate and personal tax, VAT, consultancy and tax investigation and forensics.

Some tax specialists work in personal tax compliance, completing returns for high net worth individuals with complex personal affairs. Information needs to be carefully organised and classified, and deadlines need to be met. Equally, you could be working with the trust department and preparing trust accounts and tax returns, inputting information in journals and calculating end-of-year accruals, before presenting it to clients for signature.

Others might work in global employer services, advising and managing files on executive remuneration, such as tax on directors' fees and equity-based allowances, and expatriate planning and complex equalisation processes. Additionally, you could be preparing departmental newsletters, articles and brochures.

Then again, you might work in tax depreciation, calculating tax savings for firms due to expenditure on qualifying items such as plant and machinery. Capital allowances for clients are then submitted to HM Revenue & Customs (HMRC). The work may involve site visits (to, say, airports, car dealerships, factories and offices), taking notes and photographing assets in situ, and subsequently referring to these survey results in preparing reports.

On a typical day, you would spend a great deal of time communicating by post, email and telephone and face to face, with clients and indeed with HMRC. Tax legislation is not a simple matter, so these communications can be very complex. You need to be able to argue your case clearly, convincingly and diplomatically.

The advice you give could be on starting a business or on selling property and calculating tax liable on capital gains. You might prepare and explain tax returns, and get to grips with constantly changing tax laws (you may have to read up and take courses in your own time). While the work is predominantly numerical, there is also a lot of reading and writing involved. In smaller firms, you might have a broader range of responsibilities, but in larger organisations, you are likely to specialise in one particular aspect of tax.

On the negative side, the work is very deadline-based and clients are often slow in providing the necessary information, which then places you under huge pressure, and they may then even blame you for any fines incurred! You may also need to record all your work, minute by minute, on a timesheet. You do also need to be, and consistently remain, completely up to date with the latest laws and regulations.

Once trained in practice, you could progress in professional practice to partner level, or potentially move internally to a company's tax department. Tax specialisms can be particularly lucrative.

Tolley® Exam Training

Begin your tax career with Tolley

If you're looking for a career that is challenging, varied, has a critical role in shaping the future of an organisation and is always in demand then a career in taxation is for you.

With pass rates that significantly surpass the national average and with seven training centres nationwide, it's easier than ever to gain your tax qualification with Tolley.

To view our exceptional pass rates and discover why Tolley is one of the leading national tax course providers visit www.tolley.co.uk/examtraining

 LexisNexis®   Tolley Exam Training

Profile: Tolley® Exam Training

Tolley Exam Training is one of the leading national training providers for tax qualifications. Through a combination of highly experienced tutors, quality training material and our unique online services, Tolley Exam Training offers the best study experience available. We consistently achieve exceptional pass rates which significantly surpass the national average – making us the natural choice when enrolling with a training provider to pursue a career in taxation.

Tolley Exam Training offers:

- some of the most experienced and well known tutors in the country

- a proven track record for securing outstanding pass rates

- access to Tolley's Online Academy with study manuals, audio-visual lectures and student and tutor forums, meaning you can study any time, anywhere

- Tolley's Performance Tracker, enabling you to view your study plan online and download practice exams and answers, allowing you to track your performance

- a free one-year subscription to *Taxation* magazine.

Exceptional pass rates

We consistently achieve outstanding pass rates that significantly surpass the national average and we are confident that we will continue to do so.

ATT May 2011 examinations

	Tolley Exam Training*	National average
Paper 1	94%	72%
Paper 2	97%	81%
Paper 3	100%	76%
Paper 4	100%	84%
Paper 5	100%	64%
Paper 6	94%	86%
Paper 7	96%	60%

* Students who have studied with our Guaranteed Pass Scheme

CTA May 2011 examinations

	Tolley Exam Training*	National average
Awareness	96%	91%
Advisory	79%	46%
Application	74%	44%

* Students who have studied with our Guaranteed Pass Scheme

Regional Training Centres

Due to the successful launch of our five new regional training centres, we now offer classroom training at seven locations nationwide:

- Belfast
- Birmingham
- Bristol
- Edinburgh
- London
- Manchester
- Newcastle

Qualifications offered

We are unique in the training market, being the only organisation that provides training exclusively for the professional tax examinations.

We offer training for the following examinations:

- Taxation Technician (ATT) – set by the Association of Taxation Technicians and aimed at those working in tax compliance

- Chartered Tax Adviser (CTA) – set by the Chartered Institute of Taxation and aimed at those wishing to become tax advisers

- Advanced Diploma in International Taxation (ADIT) – set by the Chartered Institute of Taxation and aimed at those who want to further their careers in international tax

- Associate of the Institute of Indirect Taxation (AIIT) – set by the Institute of Indirect Taxation and aimed at those wishing to become tax advisers in the field of indirect taxation

- VAT Compliance Diploma (VCD) – set by the Institute of Indirect Taxation and aimed at those wishing to gain an entry level qualification in, or improve their knowledge of, VAT

- ICAS Tax Qualification – set by the Institute of Chartered Accountants of Scotland and aimed at those working in a tax compliance or advisory role. It can be taken alongside the CA (Chartered Accountant) qualification or as a standalone qualification.

Innovative study system

Guaranteed Pass Scheme: our experience and previous pass rates show us that students who follow the Tolley Exam Training programme have a very high chance of passing the examinations. As a result we have introduced the Guaranteed Pass Scheme. All students enrolled with us on this programme will be given one free correspondence and revision course, in the unlikely event, they fail their examinations.

Tolley's Online Academy allows you to study any time, anywhere. You will be able to access all of our course manuals and questions banks via the Online Academy. You can view the audio visual lectures online and download the audio files of the lectures to an MP3 player.

Help is never far away through the use of the Tutor and Student Forums. The forums allow students to access our tutors' words of advice and to help build a study network by making contact with other students in different parts of the country.

The Online Academy is not only making studying more accessible for you, but it is also making it simpler by having everything you need in one place. You can even access the legislation online, by using the links in the online manuals.

Tolley's Performance Tracker allows you full access to view your study programme and track your progress by comparing it with your peers'.

For more information on Tolley Exam Training please visit www.tolley.co.uk/examtraining, email examtraining@lexisnexis.co.uk or call 020 3364 4500.

Case study

Tolley Exam Training

Claire Gallagher is a tutor at Tolley, part of LexisNexis. She can be contacted on 020 3364 4500 or at examtraining@ lexisnexis.co.uk.

Many people have a pre-conceived view of accountants (which isn't necessarily a positive one) but few people realise the variety of roles that the generic term 'accountant' encompasses. If you train as an accountant you could be working in audit, tax, corporate finance, corporate recovery, or any number of other roles which need accounting-related skills. In fact, many firms don't even refer to themselves as accountants, preferring instead the all-encompassing term 'business advisers'.

For my part I decided that I would specialise at an early age and whilst studying maths and accountancy at university I took some extra tax modules and realised how powerful knowledge of tax can be. There are two things in life that are certain, death and taxes. Tax knowledge is always going to be in demand and (believe it or not) tax is interesting!

There are people who are scared to have a go at their own taxes as it is the unknown and, if done incorrectly, can lead to serious implications. They will therefore pay someone else to do this for them. Tax is never going to get any simpler, which is why tax advisers are always in high demand.

Equally, it helps you in your personal life. Do I choose a salary package to include a company car or am I better off buying my own? By knowing the tax implications you are able to weigh up the two options. There are many work benefits where there is no tax charge, so knowledge of these is always useful.

Understanding how tax works can also save you money. For example, if I want to save money at lunchtime I would buy a cold cheese sandwich to take away, as this is a basic food item, and therefore zero-rated for VAT. Most hot food is classed as luxury items and subject to VAT at 20%, although if I have the cold cheese sandwich and 'eat in', this will then become a luxury item, so would again incur a VAT charge!

But a career in tax isn't about saving a few pounds here and there: it is about discovering opportunity and making business decisions that can literally add millions to a company's cashflow. It is not just a quirk of modern times that sees accountants being called 'business advisers'. The decisions that multinational companies make about the structure of their organisations and their subsidiaries are often based on tax. A difference in the ownership structure of a subsidiary can make a huge difference to the percentage paid in taxes on all takings. So tax advisers have a critical role to play in shaping the fortunes of organisations.

And it is not all about corporate wealth. With high net worth individuals, the opportunities become even greater and more varied. Do you invest in property, set up trust funds, place your wealth offshore in privately owned companies …? The opportunities are endless and the rewards can be startling.

To pursue in a career in tax there are many different qualifications available. These include the ATT qualification (Association of Tax Technicians), the CTA (Chartered Tax Adviser), ADIT (Advanced Diploma in International Tax) and also the more specialised indirect tax qualifications under the Institute of Indirect Tax (AIIT and VAT Compliance Diploma).

When you are looking for a job in tax, many firms will offer you the opportunity to study towards at least one of these qualifications. Some students will already have a flavour of tax from taking accountancy qualifications like the ICAS, ACCA and ICAEW.

The CTA qualification is known to represent the gold standard in UK tax education. Many students will attempt CTA after taking another qualification, not necessarily in tax. The different qualifications can be linked, as by taking previous accounting or tax qualifications you are in some cases able to obtain exemptions for part of the CTA qualification.

The tax qualifications require both the gaining of experience and the passing of examinations. Even when you have a professional qualification in tax you will need to keep up to date by taking courses, reading tax publications, and logging this with the relevant institute or association. The number of hours required and the type of learning depend on the qualification obtained.

Accounting is often misconceived as dull but in my experience it is far from it. And tax itself is anything but. When the decisions you make determine the long-term strategies of the biggest companies and most powerful people in the world, how can it be boring?

Case study

James Corcoran was a **Tax Specialist** at Deloitte

Why did you choose to work for a Big Four firm?
I chose to apply to Deloitte after reading about them in the Times Top 100 Graduate Employers. They had ranked second for a number of years and the case studies of graduates that had gone on to work for them from various backgrounds was very positive. At the time I thought it would be a fantastic opportunity to work for one of the largest and most reputable global professional services firms. It was Deloitte as a firm rather than the individual department and role that I applied for which was my original motivation.

What qualification and career route have you taken?
I am now a member of the ICAEW, having completed my ACA qualification over a three-year period whilst working at Deloitte. During this time I have worked in the corporate tax team. Prior to this I studied for a BA (Hons) degree in Geography.

What do you do on a typical day?
A typical day involves managing the ongoing compliance cycle on my clients which includes things such as computing the clients' annual corporation tax liability, filing tax returns with HMRC, calculating tax payments, liaising with HMRC and clients and researching contentious issues in the legislation. Completing the tax computation is an ongoing process throughout the year and I can be working on several clients simultaneously. I am also involved in tax advisory projects such as group restructuring or researching the impact of international tax issues.

What are the best and worst bits?
The best parts of the job are receiving praise from clients when delivering on projects or helping them achieve a significant tax saving or benefit. Working in a challenging, fast-paced and complex environment.

Worst bits: Having to complete timesheets of chargeable time, repetition of basic tasks when you are new to the job, and trying to understand tax legislation!

Do you have any tips for prospective accountants?

Be prepared: the ACA involves a lot of work and it can be difficult juggling studying with a day job.

You also need to be able to grasp technical points quickly in order to keep up with constantly changing tax legislation and rules.

What do you consider to be options open to you for the future?

Continued progression within a tax practice; this could involve moving into a particular industry sector or into a specialised area of tax, for instance R&D, transfer pricing or M&A.

Other options are to work in an in-house tax role or to move away from tax to a finance role, for instance within commerce and industry.

Corporate finance

Again, you can work in-house or in professional practice. This is primarily concerned with mergers, demergers, acquisitions and ownership change, analysis and valuation of target companies and funding of projects to set up, purchase, grow or improve the business. It may be necessary to consider and create new equity structures and shareholder bases in stock market flotations, or to restructure debt and related securities. Alternatively, it could involve financing large public sector infrastructure projects. It is one of the most dynamic, creative, strategic and exciting fields, but it is also particularly high pressure and can involve long hours. There can be a lot of people contact and negotiation with other stakeholders such as funders, bankers, lawyers, and analysts.

Corporate finance can involve corporate or private equity transactions and you could be working on either the 'buy' or 'sell' side of the deal, working with the CFO and group treasurer on transactions such as:

- mergers and acquisitions

- business disposals

- management buy-outs and buy-ins

- due diligence

- valuations

- fundraising – raising finance and flotations

- joint ventures and shareholders' agreements

- strategic and exit route planning

- reporting and transaction support.

Responsibilities might include:

- supporting the corporate finance team in the field

- preparing reports, memos, presentations and documents

- preparing financial models in Excel

- providing clients with value-adding recommendations for improvements in processes and controls

- scoping engagements, detailing budget and time frame

- drafting pitch, proposal and tender documents

- acting as point of contact in engagements

- liaising and communicating clients' feedback, and identifying and presenting potential solutions, to project managers

- assisting in preparation for and follow-up from senior meetings attended

- general correspondence, administration and billing

- collation and analysis of relevant documentation and information, drafting outputs as directed by the project manager

- producing quality schedules and appendices for reports

- supporting internal and external practice in business development

- supervising and developing junior staff.

It is possible to train in the corporate finance division of a large Public Practice, although smaller firms might start all trainees in audit. It may be more difficult to train on the client side in this specialism, because it tends to be a more experienced finance professional such as the financial director or CFO who oversees the transaction.

You could be assigned to advisory, transaction or reorganisation divisions. On the advisory side, you would be helping the client with what they should do; their best course of action, which company to buy and how to raise the finance. In transaction, you would be involved in in-depth financial analysis to decide whether the company is on a sound footing and whether or not it is an entity your client should be considering buying, or perhaps at a lower price. In reorganisation, you may be working with a struggling company, trying to organise a turnaround, or if all else fails, initiating administration proceedings.

Corporate finance is a varied field, because one day you may be meeting a target company's management and finance teams to gather information. Another day, you may be discussing transaction progress on the client's site. Then again, you may spend time in the office, checking that there is not any conflict of interests before taking on a particular transaction, performing the in-depth analysis, or drawing up the report. There may even be quieter catch-up days, and days for internal and external training. One of the satisfactions is likely to be going into a business and familiarising yourself with all aspects of its working and how it ticks, rather than focusing on just one small element, and within just a matter of days, knowing how the company works inside out and how everything fits together.

You need to present yourself well and be strong in relationship building, because there is a lot of liaison involved with different teams of accountants, lawyers and advisory personnel on both sides of the transaction. People can of course be a source of frustration in that you may be reliant on their help and unable to move on, because you are waiting for management to send some information, or lawyers to forward documentation. IT literacy is also important, as is numeracy – there is a lot of financial analysis and daily use of Excel. Do not be afraid to ask lots of questions at first, so that you are entirely sure what is being asked of you and you do not have to go back and change everything.

Salary, increasing perks and benefits, incentives and rewards can be good, and while professional, the ethos should not be too stuffy or boring; there is often a good mix of gender, age and characters, and the environment can be surprisingly open-plan, fun and chatty. With potentially 50 graduates all starting simultaneously in larger firms, you can again have an instant peer group.

Hours can be long at times, but are typically 9.00am to 6.00pm. You may have to travel, perhaps internationally, depending on where the client and target companies are situated. Some work will be completed in the office, especially if it involves particularly sensitive and privileged information.

As with all specialisms, you might progress every two to three years to the next level up, starting as an associate or trainee and then progressing through the ranks of assistant manager and manager, assistant director and director, to partner. Alternatively, you may choose to move into industry, or into banking or a private equity firm. You can move into corporate finance after starting in audit, but by starting in corporate finance you already have three years' valuable experience by the time you qualify.

> *"An economist is an expert who will know tomorrow why the things he predicted yesterday didn't happen today."*
>
> Laurence J Peter

Business recovery and insolvency

This is a Public Practice field where emotions can run high. Ideally, when a company is in financial difficulty, you will be in a position to restructure, perhaps making tough decisions to improve cashflow, renegotiate existing finances, and put the struggling firm back onto a strong footing. However, in certain instances, the company will be deemed insolvent and there will be no possible rescue strategy. As the adviser, you will need to sensitively and professionally advise on the legal and practical aspects of winding down, disposing of assets and settling debts with creditors. In such situations there is little room for sentiment and you will need to adopt a hard-headed approach.

Insolvency may be defined as when a company has cashflow difficulties and cannot pay debts as they become due, or as when it has a balance sheet deficit between net assets and debts. Thus, a firm may be cashflow insolvent but balance sheet solvent, should it have sufficient illiquid assets. The reverse may also be true, should it have a balance sheet deficit but strong cashflow (many firms operate in this state without default, due to circumstances such as bank loans and investor funding). To be insolvent, the firm has to be deemed both cashflow and balance sheet insolvent.

New legislation encourages restructuring and remodelling of finances to enable the business to continue, but in certain instances liquidation will be the only solution. To give the firm time to restructure and recover, it may be placed in administration, which provides temporary protection from creditors. Voluntary arrangements may then be made with creditors to accept regular monthly payments and perhaps agree to write off part of the debt. As an insolvency specialist, you would manage all this. You would advise clients on how to reorganise corporate entities, realise or dispose of assets, settle creditor claims and distribute surplus to shareholders.

Each company's situation will be different and you may be the first point of contact in engagements, responsible for handling statutory requirements, and for writing reports and liaising with creditors regarding the progress in the voluntary or compulsory administration process. The work is varied; you may be on site, dealing with customers, suppliers and other stakeholders, or in the office, investigating directors' conduct in the case of insolvency (directors are not allowed to continue running a firm they know to be in trouble). The business could be of any type and industry (consumer goods, energy, financial services, real estate, manufacturing, telecommunications, leisure and so on), and there can be surprises. As we have seen recently, even seemingly well-established firms can quickly collapse in an economic downturn (for example, Northern Rock, MFI, Dolphin Bathrooms and Woolworths).

Obviously, it is not only businesses that become insolvent, and in certain instances you may be dealing with bankruptcy of individuals, again calling for great empathy and sensitivity, while maintaining a pragmatic and professional stance.

> *"About the time we can make the ends meet, somebody moves the ends."*
>
> Herbert Hoover

Forensic accounting

In Public Practice, forensic accounting involves 'detective' investigation in fraud, divorce and personal injury cases. It means logically looking for clues and anomalies in often vast amounts of complex and 'hidden' financial data, and collating and presenting findings, perhaps as an expert witness in court. This plays to accounting and legal knowledge, but also calls for understanding of IT systems and skills and sensitivity in interviewing. As a forensic accountant, you might work for law firms, the police, Public Practice firms, banks and government agencies.

However, the work can sometimes feel like a thankless task. In spite of some personal satisfaction in solving the puzzle and proving 'how it was done and by whom', when you uncover a major fraud and loss to a company, the organisation can be embarrassed and keen to cover up rather than heralding you as the hero. That said, external stakeholders should appreciate your efforts.

Forensic accountants specialise in the financial models, tools and techniques, and the systems expertise and technologies, to gather evidence to globally accepted standards. As the 'detectives' of the financial world, they are often multi-qualified and trained to look for anomalies and hidden clues. As a forensic accountant you might also consider patterns of human behaviour, follow trails left by economic transactions, or search and recover electronic records (whether lost through accident or deliberately), to find the true facts or correct financial value.

You would routinely investigate insurance claims, corporate transactions and civil disputes such as divorce, or criminal disputes, like fraud. You would place value on assets for business funding, operation or liquidation, and delve into public sector losses, fraud and compliance or governance issues. You might further act as an expert witness in court proceedings.

Financial controller

This is an internal operational role, primarily concerned with cashflow and efficiency, timeliness of payments to and from the firm, and day-to-day management of the finance function. You need to be systematic and organised, but with an eye on the bigger picture and payments in the pipeline.

This is often the stepping stone to the role of financial director and it is a senior pivotal role in a company where you will be involved in all major business decisions and acquisitions. You are likely to have managerial responsibility for the bookkeeping and administrative staff; indeed, this may be the first experience of people management on a large scale. It is important to foster a climate of mutual respect. A disciplinarian approach is no longer acceptable and you will need to develop softer people skills, which may not always come naturally to more 'black or white' types (who may be typically drawn to accounting).

Financial controllers head up financial activities, from analysis, to reporting, to more strategic involvement. It is a hands-on role, concerned with cashflow, accounts production, target setting, departmental monitoring, auditing and oversight of tax and regulatory and compliance issues, to ensure efficiency and best practice.

Your responsibilities might include:

- developing effective systems and procedures

- creating frameworks for financial control, accountability and authority

- developing efficient and secure central accounting system

- liaising with and informing external auditors

- ensuring adherence to group policies and accounting standards

- providing recommendations for financial improvement or control

- drafting of statutory accounts for the group.

"A budget tells us what we can't afford, but it doesn't keep us from buying it."

William Feather

Financial director

Financial directors work in-house and take a senior and influential role and adopt the ultimate responsibility for financial strategies and risks. They oversee, change and take responsibility for financial analysis, planning and reporting at senior and board level. As the name suggests, they direct and shape the finance function and impact on the senior decision-making of the company.

Obviously, duties will depend, somewhat, on the company size and the laws of the country it is in, but as the financial director you would oversee all financial aspects of company strategy, and flow of information to the CEO, board and external stakeholders such as investors and banks.

You will need to build your own team, whether capitalising on available talent or bringing in new blood. It is common for FDs to take their 'right-hand man' with them when they move jobs – they need to have a 'safe pair of hands' whom they can trust to deal with the day-to-day operations. As an FD, you need to be relieved of the hands-on responsibility, so that you might concentrate on the broader picture and strategy.

Your responsibilities generally include:

- overall control of a business's financial strategy, and planning, managing, evaluating and reporting, including development of policies, systems, processes

- compliance-consistent reporting and accounting, including taxation, dividends, annual report and accounts

- analysing sales projections and income against actual figures and suggesting improvements to the planning process

- assessing long-term financial trends and reviewing prospects for future growth of income and new product areas (with the board)

- oversight of financial communications strategy, e.g. stock market, business press and business analysts' community

- recruitment, selection, training, motivation and management of financial personnel

- strategic planning and development (with the executive team), and perhaps recording and disseminating information and reports to executive and management teams

- perhaps, additionally, company insurance, import/export administration, licensing, legal areas and activities, corporate level negotiations, (e.g. regarding premises, plant, trading, acquisitions and divestments, disposals), contracts and agreements, major supplier/customer/partner relationships, regulatory body relationships, approvals and accreditations

- some IT responsibilities

- some environmental/sustainability and CSR responsibilities

- some quality assurance or health and safety responsibilities

- company secretary/corporate finance responsibilities should there not be an appointed company secretary or treasurer (e.g. statutory company, capital requirements, debt, equity and mergers and acquisitions administration)

- company director responsibilities, if appropriate.

"If you owe the bank $100 that's your problem. If you owe the bank $100 million, that's the bank's problem."

J Paul Getty

Management accounting

Most management accountants work in-house, but there can be opportunities in the advisory divisions of Public Practice. Management accounting involves taking a broader perspective on the business, liaising with different business functions on resourcing issues. As a management accountant you would generate regular internal reports, which enable the managers to monitor performance, forecast and plan appropriately. You might advise on the financial implications of projects, explain the financial consequences of earlier decisions, monitor and control finances, or conduct internal audits and devise strategy in the light of the competitive landscape.

The role of management accountant is increasingly as a business partner to the line managers, ensuring that they have accurate, timely and relevant information to aid their decision-making and planning. You would act as a change agent, evaluating existing measures and procedures, and making recommendations for improvements.

Your typical responsibilities might be:

- managing a team in the production of management accounts

- advising and supporting senior executives and directors, and producing weekly, monthly and quarterly management reports

- evaluating productivity models, analysing budget variances and exploring potential problems with line managers – it is important to build strong and positive working relationships with departmental heads, because you will need these people on your side

- developing and revising strategic plans and recommendations for business improvement and innovation

- preparing tax returns, statements of cashflow, and income and expenditure accounts

- appraising and improving financial information systems informing budgets, forecasts and business planning

- controlling financial expenditure and establishing and maintaining costing models

- project planning and resourcing, pre-empting potential problems or opportunities

- any ad hoc research and analysis with commentary and conclusions

- helping the company to comply with industry regulations.

Unlike in financial accounting, management accounting is less concerned with retrospective, historic data and more concerned with the future. It is more 'big picture', and timeliness is arguably more important than the pinpoint accuracy of audited financial statements (indeed, management accountants are not qualified to audit in Public Practice). As a management accountant, you would not be confined by traditional accounting practices, but could delve into operational research and other economic and statistical models. You might focus more on individual aspects of the business and on areas such as market, product and sales trends. It could be exciting if you like to think quickly on your feet and to find innovative solutions, but a perfectionist may find management accountancy too imprecise and prescient.

> *"The man who will use his skill and constructive imagination to see how much he can give for a dollar, instead of how little he can give for a dollar, is bound to succeed."*
>
> *Henry Ford*

Financial analyst

In both internal and practice roles, financial analysis can be quite quantitative, because you are looking for evidence that something is working or not, or that it would or would not be a viable proposition. Often the projects are bespoke, but there may be some more routine reporting as well. Financial analysts work in all industries, such as retail, FMCGs, property, banking and financial services, software, telecommunications, oil and entertainment.

Financial analysis involves delving into the detail of what is really happening financially. You need to collate and analyse data, identify trends and make recommendations for significant changes, which optimise pricing and processes, minimise costs and waste, and produce measurable benefits. At junior level, the hard analysis and factual research and verification will be your responsibility, whereas planning and decision-making on the basis of findings will be the job of more senior financial analysts.

Your typical responsibilities would include:

- analysis of reports from sales, marketing, purchasing, production and communication divisions (you will perhaps be the main interface between finance and these divisions), and using statistical software and spreadsheets, producing your own reports and making recommendations for continuous improvement

- undertaking research, identifying trends, risks and opportunities, variance and anomalies, and perhaps performing peer or competitor analysis, to formulate accurate forecasts

- keeping up to date with and developing new tools, models, indicators and techniques for financial planning and forecasting

- reporting on organic changes, challenging assumptions, and liaising with senior decision-makers to evaluate and monitor the impact of planned interventions and changes, devised to improve efficiency and measurable performance

- in a financial institution, extracting information to gain insight into a company's prospects and managerial effectiveness, and advising on investment decisions.

Financial analysis can be varied and stimulating, and through reading between the lines, and performing your own research, quantitative analysis and modelling, you can unearth some interesting and useful information about the realities of the company's, peer's or competitor's financial situation, functioning and direction. It provides scope for a kind of corporate espionage, detective work and creativity, for fact-finding and generating innovative and practical solutions and recommendations, both strategic and operational.

Financial analysis can be both retrospective and forward-thinking. It is not always focused on spreadsheets and balance sheets, and the project work provides variety and a clear focus. However, financial analysis may be frustrating in that you are ultimately not in control and making the decisions yourself, and it will be up to someone else whether they choose to listen to and act on your advice, investing or withdrawing, actually implementing your recommendations or simply filing your hard work to be forgotten in a filing cabinet!

> *"Definition of a statistician: a man who believes figures don't lie, but admits than under analysis some of them won't stand up either. "*
>
> *Evan Esar*

2

Overview of the professional bodies

The key professional bodies and qualifications

The qualification and route into accountancy that you choose should be a matter of personal preference and circumstances. It helps to consider why accountancy appeals in the first place. What particular financial specialisms are most attractive and why? In what sort of company or sector you could see yourself working? Where you could see yourself going in the longer term? It is important to carefully research the options available for study, the syllabuses and emphases of different qualifications, the types of accountancy firms and settings, and their different ethos, requirements and opportunities.

You also need to consider what you represent as a human resource: your motivations, abilities and personal qualities. It can be helpful to have someone who knows you well offer an opinion on which area of accountancy they believe would suit you best, but equally, you could seek more objective advice from a professional career consultant, who may have psychometric tools to help inform your decision. Such considerations, and resultant self-awareness, clarity and focus, should ensure that you make the correct choices and should serve you well in selection interviews.

What are the primary professional qualifications and what is the difference between them? There are four main distinct examining bodies, which will be discussed in detail in this chapter.

1. ICAEW (Institute of Chartered Accountants in England and Wales) which has Scottish (ICAS) and Irish (ICAI) equivalents.

2. ACCA (Association of Chartered Certified Accountants).

3. CIMA (Chartered Institute of Management Accountants).

4. CIPFA (Chartered Institute of Public Finance and Accountancy).

There is also the AAT (Association of Accounting Technicians), which is a standalone award, but often used as a foundation qualification for the above professional qualifications. We will discuss this in chapter 5.

The Professional Oversight Board's 2011 survey report 'Key Facts and Trends in the Accountancy Profession' lists the 304,000 qualified accountants in the UK, and 424,000 globally, under qualifying body. It also provides data on sector and gender by percentage. Figures are from December 2010.

TABLE 4: Members of accountancy professional bodies

	UK members	Worldwide members	% practice	% industry & commerce	% public sector	% women
ACCA	72,565	144,397	26	56	10	44
CIMA	66,342	83,487	1	73	16	31
CIPFA	13,297	13,668	3	8	63	30
ICAEW	115,990	136,615	32	42	4	25
ICAI	18,145	20,010	31	57	4	36
ICAS	16,270	18,780	29	41	3	30
AIA	1,674	7,046	5	84	1	28
	304,283	424,003				

N.B. AIA are members of the Association of International Accountants: www.aiaworldwide.com
Source: POB

Trainee representation of different professional bodies in Public Practice 2011

Accountancy magazine's annual survey of the top 60 firms found that in 2011 there were 8,000 ICAEW trainees (63%), 2,700 ICAS trainees (21%), 1,600 ACCA students (13%), 160 CIMA students (1%) and 84 trainees taking the CIPFA qualification (1%).

In the Big Four, the proportions are 62% ICAEW, 27% ICAS, 9% ACCA, 2% CIMA and 1% CIPFA. Clearly, this means that the vast majority (84%) in the top 60 Public Practice firms are in reality ACA/CA (chartered accountancy) trainees.

While the ICAEW maintains its position as having the largest number of UK members, ACCA and CIMA have shown the greatest increase in numbers over the last five years, and the ACCA has the highest representation globally.

CIMA (1%) and CIPFA (3%) are the lowest represented in professional practice, compared with nearly one third of all ICAEW members (including non-working members or those working in 'other' fields such as a professional body). Perhaps by definition, CIMA has the highest proportion of members working in industry and commerce (nearly three quarters), and CIPFA in the public sector (nearly two thirds). Figures do not total 100% because some members are retired, currently unemployed, or working in none of the above organisations.

Popularity among the sexes

Proportionally, ACCA has the highest percentage of women (44%), compared with just 25% who are ICAEW members. This is not explicable by women preferring internal roles, because then you would expect to see an even higher proportion of CIMA-qualified women.

ACCA has always encouraged women; it was the first professional body to welcome Ethel Ayres Purdie, one of the first female accountants, in 1909.

In 1971, Vera di Palma made history as the first ACCA council member and then in 1980, the first female president. ACCA scored another first, when Anthea Rose became ACCA's first chief executive and indeed the first of any professional accountancy body in the world, holding the position for a decade.

In 2007, after a period as finance director with the University of Birmingham, Gill Ball had the privilege of being elected president of the ACCA council, but she was still only the third female to hold this position; for the other 26 years, ACCA had a male president. Helen Brand, CEO since 2008, says that ACCA challenges the establishment and focuses on talent and ambition, making it inspiring and meritocratic. Brand believes that the ACCA culture of customer service and the role of accountants in creating and managing the economic upturn (in due course) will provide excellent prospects for accountants, an increasing number of whom will be women.

Institute of Chartered Accountants in England and Wales: ICAEW (ACA)

The ICAEW (www.icaew.com) was established by Royal Charter in 1880 and has in excess of 136,000 members worldwide and 116,000 in the UK. The ICAEW represents Chartered Accountants and oversees the ACA qualification.

ACA is arguably perceived as the most prestigious and competitive of the accountancy qualifications and it has been reported that the majority of financial directors in FTSE companies are ACA-qualified, many through Big Four firms. It is a rigorous and sought-after qualification in business as well as in banking and finance.

Chartered Accountants act as business advisers. They aim to maximise profitability and to inform high-level strategic decisions, which will increase market share for client companies. They undertake audits and provide financial reports and information, and may specialise in insolvency, audit, taxation, corporate finance,

Figure 1: Main accountancy bodies.

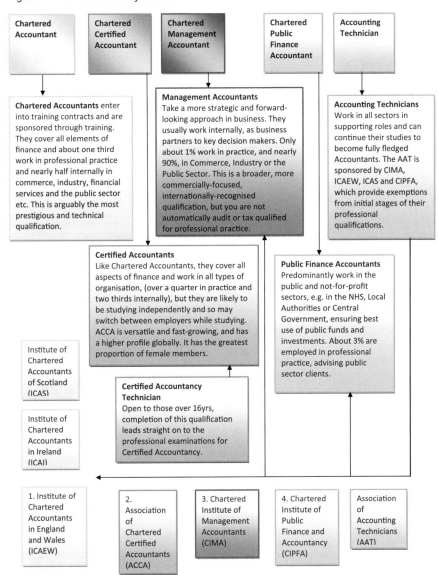

treasury, forensic accounting or accounting systems. The majority of training opportunities are in Public Practice, but there are increasing opportunities in industry. After qualifying, they may choose to work in-house, in any industrial, corporate, public or not-for-profit sector.

Typically, Chartered Accountants spend time liaising with clients and providing financial information and advice, reviewing company systems, and performing checks to analyse risk. They advise on transactions like mergers and acquisitions, insolvency, tax and fraud, besides managing junior colleagues. In internal roles, they may produce reports and recommendations following liaison with internal and external auditors, preparing statements, reports and accounts. They may take responsibility for planning, forecasting and perhaps negotiating with suppliers and creditors, too.

The ICAEW promotes chartered accountancy as affording great variety, challenge, excitement and security, and as being an excellent route to a very rewarding career in business leadership. Learning while earning, you will be highly marketable with a good income, and your salary should double on qualification. ACA has the highest pass rate (not necessarily the easiest examinations – the success may reflect the calibre of students and the level of support afforded to trainees), and undoubtedly it provides the credibility and marketability for the most senior positions (more CEOs, CFOs and chairpersons are qualified in ACA than any other professional body). Career choices on qualification are endless. The POB survey 2011 found 32% of members to be in Public Practice.

ACA is a two-stage qualification. You will be earning well, but study on top of a full workload can be very demanding. In the initial Professional Stage, you study technical knowledge modules and core competencies underpinning accountancy, combined with a more applied, practical element; that is, work experience advising and problem-solving in various scenarios. The subsequent Advanced Stage involves two more complex technical papers and a case study. ACA is often purported to be more intellectually demanding than the ACCA route, and you are committed to the employer to whom you are contracted, so you cannot change employer mid-studies.

I AM THE FUTURE CEO OF...

THE CHARTERED ACCOUNTANT.
NO ONE'S BETTER QUALIFIED.

Ambition's a funny thing. Simply having it isn't enough; knowing what to do with it really makes the difference. That's why no one trains to be an ICAEW Chartered Accountant by accident. And it's certainly no accident 84% of FTSE 100 companies have an ICAEW Chartered Accountant on their board. How far will your ambition take you?

Start writing your future. Visit icaew.com/betterqualified

ICAEW

Profile: ICAEW

Opportunity, variety and the ability to work in any industry, anywhere in the world, are just some of the benefits of becoming an ICAEW Chartered Accountant.

Whether it's giving business advice to a high street retail chain, testifying as an expert witness in court or ensuring the business sustainability of a multinational organisation, Chartered Accountants are vital to the success of any organisation.

Being 'chartered' means you are recognised as being at the top of your chosen profession. It shows you have the industry-specific skills and experience, not just the academic and theoretical knowledge.

No-one's better qualified

There's no denying a career in business is competitive. That's why ICAEW train chartered accountants to have the skills and expertise the business world demands. Choosing the ACA qualification will be your ticket to a successful and lucrative career, full of global opportunities.

This combination of skill and expertise is why ICAEW members work at the highest levels. They are the finance directors, CEOs and partners of some of the world's largest organisations.

Did you know: 84% of FTSE 100 companies have at least one ICAEW Chartered Accountant on their board?

Your route to success

To become an ICAEW Chartered Accountant, you will need to complete the ACA qualification. The ACA is a professional business and finance qualification, which means it is a combination of practical on-the-job work experience, technical learning and exams. This integrated approach ensures you have the technical knowledge and practical ability you need, in order to demonstrate to employers and clients throughout your career that you have the skills and expertise to be valuable to their organisation, whichever sector they are in.

You can start training for the ACA at a number of stages in your education. There are a number of school leaver opportunities available, you can decide to start after a qualification such as the AAT or the Certificate in Finance, Accounting and Business or as a graduate.

Depending on the programme you choose, it should take between three and five years to qualify as an ACA. You study for the ACA while you are working, starting salaries are competitive and will generally increase throughout your training.

Once you've qualified, the opportunities are endless; you can work in any sector of business, anywhere in the world.

Case study

We caught up with William and Bradley to see where the ACA has taken their career.

William, ACA, Chief Executive, York Racecourse

"For the past eight years I have been Chief Executive and Clerk of the Course at York Racecourse, one of Europe's leading horse racing venues. It perfectly combines my passion for sport with my fascination for business and figures. In fact, this is probably the closest I will come to my 'dream job'.

"A degree in agricultural economics, then training with PricewaterhouseCoopers in Cambridge, took me to Ascot Racecourse.

"Being involved in both sport and a business which has broad elements including media rights, betting and venue management is exciting, challenging and thoroughly rewarding.

"My tip for anyone wanting an interesting career in their particular passion is to acquire sound, globally recognised business skills which they can then bring with their talents to that industry.

"Consider the doors which a first-class qualification like chartered accountancy will open, where it could take you – and what a firm bedrock it will prove in the future."

Bradley, Brentnalls SA (Australia)

"I wanted to be a pilot when I was younger but when I got to college I was pretty sure accountancy and finance was what I wanted to do. I chose the ACA as it was the logical step following my AAT qualification. It's a well respected qualification known all over the world and allows AAT students to continue their professional development.

"It has taken me from a medium-sized accountancy practice to a FTSE 100 company in Vodafone plc and now I'm working overseas."

To find out where the ACA and a career as an ICAEW Chartered Accountant can take you, visit icaew.com/careers or the Facebook fan page facebook.com/icaewstartingpoint.

Scotland and Ireland

For chartered accountancy qualifications in Scotland and Ireland, the relevant bodies are respectively:

Institute of Chartered Accountants of Scotland (www.icas.org.uk)

It is also possible to study for this Scottish qualification in the rest of the UK. For example, Ernst & Young favours ICAS because examinations are 'front-loaded'; you cram at college early on to accelerate a strong technical foundation.

Founded in 1854, the ICAS is the original accountancy body and it pioneered International Accounting Standards. It is the fastest-growing accountancy body (with a 94% growth rate). ICAS both trains and examines, leading to high standards. It trains more graduates than any other body (96%–94% with at least a 2.i), and only ICAS members can use the label CA (Chartered Accountant): others use the designation ACA.

Institute of Chartered Accountants of Ireland (www.icai.ie)

With about 20,000 members and over 5,000 students, the ICAI is the leading voice for chartered accountancy in both the Republic of Ireland and Northern Ireland. Established by Royal Charter in 1888, ICAI is the largest and longest established accountancy body in Ireland. Members are bound by its handbook of rules regarding professionalism and ethics.

Represented in over 80 countries, 65% of members work internally in finance, business and industry and the other 35% work in professional practice, advising a wide variety of clients.

What are the ACA entry requirements?

It is possible to enter chartered accountancy as a school leaver with A levels or an AAT (Association of Accounting Technicians) qualification, but in reality 80% of trainees are graduates. Indeed, many training employers will not only demand at least 2.i honours, but also a UCAS tariff above 280 (usually higher), and you are likely to be put through a rigorous selection procedure involving psychometric tests, role plays and interviews. Smaller firms may accept an applicant with 2.ii honours, but 87% of graduate ACA trainees have a first or 2.i honours. The gender balance is around 45% female and 55% male.

Does it matter what degree you have?

Mathematics at A level is not a prerequisite; nor is a business, accounting, economics or finance degree, although in reality such studies and evidence of commercial understanding and experience will be viewed favourably.

About half the 2009–10 graduate ACA intake had a business or finance degree, and one quarter had science, mathematics and engineering qualifications, but this may be more to do with self-selection (accountancy appeals to such facts and figures-oriented people) than any recruitment bias. Should your degree be relevant, you may be able to gain credits towards professional qualifications.

For school leaver entry, two A levels (often in 'solid academic' subjects other than, say, general studies) and three GCSEs with A/B grades in English and mathematics at GCSE, are required, or the International Baccalaureate (IB) or BTEC National Diploma equivalent.

The AAT-ACA fast track affords credits towards professional qualifications, which means that A level to ACA can take you just four years.

Other skills you need

After the war, American comedian Bob Newhart took a job as an accountant. He later claimed that his motto, 'That's close enough', and his habit of adjusting petty cash imbalances with his own money shows he didn't exactly have the temperament to be an accountant!

Firms will also be looking for evidence of:

- self-discipline and commitment (to combine the demands of work and study)

- analytical and problem-solving skills

- people and communication skills

- integrity and trustworthiness

- numeracy and IT literacy

- organisational skills and time management

- initiative and independence

- team-working and perhaps leadership potential

- flexibility, confidence and drive.

Possible career progression

For the first three years, you will gain experience and adopt more responsibility with the training employer to whom you are contracted. You may take on more client-facing and supervisory duties (although with smaller firms you may be dealing with clients from an earlier stage).

Post-qualification, the opportunities greatly increase. You could stay in professional practice, perhaps transferring to different specialisms, taking secondments abroad and broadening experience, or simply move up the management ladder with a view to becoming a senior manager after about five years and eventually a partner (eight to 15 years). You might join a smaller or larger firm, or even go self-employed in the longer term.

Then again, many Chartered Accountants make a move in-house (according to POB figures, about half work internally in banking, industry, commerce, public or voluntary sectors). Typically, you would start in internal audit, financial accounting or business analysis immediately after qualifying, although more managerial roles open up with longer experience. It is possible to make finance director within 10 to 15 years, although due to their comprehensive business training, many Chartered Accountants eventually take broader general management, chairman and CEO roles.

The working environment

The working environment is formal and you will be expected to wear a suit and to maintain a professional image, at least when client-facing (some will allow you to dress down when in the office). However, do ensure that you do not allow the formality to stifle your own personality – clients really hate having to deal with a 'dull' auditor.

You are likely to be contracted to work overtime on demand, particularly from January to March, the busiest period for audit. Indeed, hours may be extremely long during this period, especially when working for financial services clients in the City. You do need to do this overtime and to demonstrate a positive attitude towards it; the quickest way to lose the support of your managers and peers is by not contributing to the team effort. That said, you may need to learn to say no at times, for the sake of your sanity.

Your work will also demand substantial travel to clients' premises. All your expenses will be reimbursed, but for London auditors working in financial services, you may well stay in hotels around the country for many weeks at a time, returning home just at weekends. If you are interested in international travel, it is sensible to apply to firms with overseas offices to which you might be seconded.

Typical salaries and employee benefits

Starting salaries vary greatly according to the size and location of the firm, and the sector. As you might expect, pay tends to be higher in London and the south-east.

Figures for 2011 on the ICAEW site show that as an ACA, you might earn on average £45,000 in the first two years after qualification, rising to £66,000 six to nine years after qualification, and peaking at £88,000 after 10 to 20 years.

Londoners earn an average basic of £92,000, approximately £7,000 more than other southern regions and about £20,000 to £30,000 more than northern counties, no doubt partly due to the higher representation of banking and capital markets, and insurance (which are significantly higher paid sectors).

Main additional benefits include bonus (averaging from £1,600 in early years to as much as £22,000 after 10 to 20 years), pension, health care, life assurance, car allowances, and share options, but may include leisure facilities, optional holiday, career development, sabbaticals, study support and flexitime. Larger firms often afford a personal 'benefits budget', which you may use to 'purchase' your preferred options (such as extra holiday, coaching or childcare vouchers), or simply a cash pay-out on top of salary. Additionally, while studying, study support and a 'no overtime' agreement may be granted.

Profile: Newcastle University Business School

Life in the fast track

In 2010, a brand new qualification was developed by the ICAEW and Newcastle University Business School.

The Graduate Diploma in Finance, Accounting and Business is a new route into finance, providing students with both a Graduate Diploma and the CFAB, as well as seven of the 15 papers required to qualify as a Chartered Accountant. Here, Lauren Campbell gives her thoughts on being in the first cohort.

Why did you choose to study at Newcastle?

"I was attracted to Newcastle University because of its excellent reputation, particularly the Business School as it has strong links with the ICAEW. Newcastle is also a great city to live in with friendly people and a vibrant nightlife."

Why did you choose the Graduate Diploma in Finance, Accounting and Business?

"It has so much to offer, especially for those who want to cross into accountancy from a non-business background. The Business School's experience in developing students and the ICAEW's involvement are invaluable assets guaranteed to kick-start a professional career. Another appealing aspect is the seven exemptions, which are vital in setting you apart as the ideal candidate for a firm to hire."

What aspects did you most enjoy?

"I have enjoyed the personal and professional skills element. The interactive sessions allowed me to learn from experts and my peers in order to develop the skills required to become a successful professional. It's aspects like this that make the Graduate Diploma a rare and exciting opportunity."

What are your career ambitions?

"I'm aiming to become a Chartered Accountant within the next three to four years. The degree has already helped me start working towards this goal – I've received an offer for a training contract with an accountancy firm where I can complete the rest of the exams necessary to become a Chartered Accountant."

Newcastle University Business School is currently recruiting for next September's intake.

The view from ICAEW

"We have had close links with Newcastle University Business School for a number of years and its Graduate Diploma provides a new and innovative way for students to progress with their academic studies and make progress towards the ICAEW's ACA qualification. Successful graduates from the scheme will help make themselves much more attractive to employers." Shaun Robertson, Head of Learning, ICAEW

For further information about the programme, please contact Ellen Thomson (ellen.thomas@ncl.ac.uk) or Lorna Hansell (lorna.hansell@icaew.com).

Association of Chartered Certified Accountants (ACCA)

The Association of Chartered Certified Accountants (ACCA; www.accaglobal.com) is the largest and perhaps fastest-growing global accountancy professional body. It has 400,000 students and over 140,000 members in 170 countries.

The Big Four do offer this highly respected qualification stream as well, but ACCA affords greater flexibility than ACA, in that you might work for any finance department while studying, and you can switch jobs should you wish. Many trainees do train with one of the 8,500 ACCA-approved employers around the world, but this is not essential. It has been suggested that ACCA is more internationally recognised (it is a global body, rather than UK-centred, particularly focused on 'professional values, ethics and governance'). That said, ACCA also purports to understand the real issues facing small businesses, and 63,000 of their members work in SMEs or small partnerships worldwide. High street accountants to the public are often ACCA-qualified. Competition is again very fierce, especially in large financial blue chips and for industry positions affording good packages for study, so early application in a final degree year is advised.

ACCA accountants develop and maintain financial and accounting systems and records, and they provide financial forecasts, as well as auditing and investigating any irregularities. They focus on maximising profitability and efficiency whether working internally or for a client organisation, and they may choose to specialise, in, for instance, insolvency, tax and corporate finance. Pressure can be particularly high at financial year, quarter and month ends. Many large corporations have to submit quarterly updates to their brokers, to ensure the financial markets are informed about the firm's progress. They are found in all sectors (public, commercial, and industrial, and financial services) and in professional practice (56% in commercial fields, 26% in Public Practice and the remaining 10% in the public sector).

The 14 examinations need to be passed within 10 years, but there is no time limit for gaining the required three years' practical work experience (although all accountancy studies are easier if you are actually performing relevant work). Thirteen performance objectives need to be monitored and met by an appointed workplace mentor, but this could be before, after or during studies. The technical areas covered by both ACA and ACCA exams are said to be similar. ACA perhaps places more emphasis on case studies and analysis at the final stage.

So what are the advantages of ACCA? ACCA is a global qualification based on international accounting standards, but also tailored to incorporate and test knowledge of legal and tax regulations in your own country. ACCA is perhaps less technically specific and is relevant and applicable to all sectors, whether professional practice, or finance departments in corporate or public sector arenas. The only professional body with a mandatory ethics module, ACCA has recognised the increasing concern for professionalism and corporate social responsibility in today's world. Additionally, the flexible approach to CPD ensures development and continuous learning is personally relevant and of practical value, as well as suited to your lifestyle and active involvements (for example, classroom and conference courses, on-the-job learning, committee membership).

Finally, uniquely to ACCA, the two final modules enable you to choose specialist papers most relevant to your career aspirations (advanced financial management/ performance management/taxation/audit and assurance).

What are the ACCA entry requirements?

Is a degree essential?

Officially, no degree or HND (BTEC Higher National Diploma) is essential, but in reality preference will be given to the highest qualified. While you may enter from any discipline, the following degree/HND subjects are viewed favourably:

- accountancy and finance

- international business; business and management

- mathematics

- economics

- languages, increasingly.

Again, 2.i honours are predominantly required, together with strong A levels, and English and mathematics at GCSE. As an ACCA graduate trainee, you may claim up to nine exemptions from the ACCA examinations, should your degree studies be relevant.

For school leaver registration with the ACCA, you must be over 18 years old, with two A levels and three GCSEs, including English and mathematics and in five distinct subjects.

Mature students need to be over 21 years, but require no formal academic qualifications. However, to progress to the ACCA, you do have just a two-year window to pass the first two papers (F1 and F2).

Other skills needed

Personal motivations, traits and skills required include:

- commercial understanding and a general business interest
- self-discipline and commitment (to combine the demands of work and study)
- analytical and problem-solving skills
- interpersonal and communication skills
- integrity and trustworthiness
- numeracy and IT literacy
- organisational and time management skills, and attention to detail
- initiative, proactivity and independence
- team-working and perhaps leadership potential.

Increasingly, employers also look for relevant experience, whether work shadowing, temping, internships or holiday jobs. In today's competitive market, you need strong and solid evidence that you want to, and can, do the work and fit in.

Possible career progression

The practical experience element of training ensures both breadth and depth of experience, and once ACCA-qualified, you might progress further by taking greater supervisory responsibility and more complex and prestigious clients and projects. You can be awarded a lot of responsibility at an early stage, and this develops increasingly from performing operational financial tasks to taking a more strategic role (depending on individual preferences and ambitions). The broad ACCA syllabus and strategic emphasis also equips you for a wider commercial role and you might subsequently move into general or operational management, and even strategy and consultancy positions.

Alternatively, you may choose to specialise, in, say, audit, risk or forensic accounting. There is an expectation that you will actively ensure that your knowledge and skill set remain current and in tune with today's business needs.

In Private Practice, you might expect to reach partner level within 10 years, or you might obtain a practising certificate of your own and set up your own practice or work as a sole trader.

The working environment

As we have seen, 50% of ACCA members work in the corporate sector, 26% in professional and Public Practice and 10% in public sector arenas. You might work anywhere in the world, because the qualification is offered and recognised in more than 170 countries.

Companies of all sizes and in all industries (ranging from aerospace, telecommunications and transport to pharmaceuticals and food), and every sector (commercial and financial services such as retail, hospitality, banking and insurance, and public sector, charitable and not-for-profit concerns like the NHS, local authorities, educational institutions and NGOs), train and employ ACCA members. Settings are typically formal in major national and international companies, and in client-facing Public Practice roles, but smaller concerns may accept smart casual attire and suits may not always be obligatory.

Chartered certified accountants generally work a normal 35- to 40-hour week, but you may need to work longer hours or at weekends during peak times or to meet a particular client's pressing need. You may need to travel to clients' premises in audit, which could necessitate significant periods away from home. International secondments are often also available in multinationals.

It is suggested that 39% of ACCA members are afforded flexible working arrangements, with 21% able to work from home.

Typical salaries and benefits

As with other fields of accountancy, starting salaries vary greatly according to size and type of firm, location (highest being in London and the City), qualifications and sector (financial services being the most lucrative), but range between £15,000 and £25,000, and then £30,000 to £52,000 after qualification. After 10 years and when working at more senior level, you might command £40,000 to £100,000.

Your other benefits might include pension, health insurance, profit-share, car allowances and bonus.

Profile: ACCA

Climb higher with ACCA

As the global body for professional accountants, ACCA offers you more. More than just a good reputation. More than worldwide influence and career progress in any organisation. ACCA offers you the world.

Qualifying with ACCA is your first step towards a successful career in accountancy, business and finance. The breadth of the ACCA Qualification makes it the perfect platform to launch any business career, and you will have the opportunity to acquire the technical skills that employers are now demanding. Our qualification gives you the transferable skills you need, so that in the long term you can apply for finance roles in any sector, in any business, anywhere in the world.

ACCA's flexible approach means freedom. Internships at university can count towards the practical experience requirements of the qualification and enhance your employability. Also, exemptions from a relevant degree mean fewer exams to sit. As the contract isn't tied into a training contract, you can take your hard work with you whenever you move jobs. The ACCA Qualification really does give you freedom, recognition and the power to choose your own career path in accountancy, business and finance.

There are three equally important elements to qualifying as an ACCA accountant – exams, practical experience and an online ethics module. The exams are progressive, so if you have a degree in history or economics you will build on your knowledge as you progress. If you have a relevant degree you'll likely be entitled to some exemptions, and will enter the qualification at the most appropriate level.

ACCA is the largest and fastest growing international accountancy body, with over 404,000 students and 140,000 members in 170 countries. Studying with ACCA allows you to build a future that is diverse, challenging and full of opportunities.

Start your journey today at www.accaglobal.com/uk/join

Case study

Audits, Advice and ACCA

Helen Gunnell, Audit Executive at Ernst & Young LLP (Nottingham), knew that the ACCA Qualification would open doors and give her the knowledge she needed to pursue a career in accountancy.

"My strengths are in numerical-based subjects. Therefore when I left university I worked in a bank and then a regional building society. After a few years I wanted a challenge in my career," says Helen, who decided that the ACCA Qualification was the right path for her.

After completing a BA Honours degree in Economics, she was encouraged by her employers to undertake the ACCA Qualification. "I was excited to be offered a position with the firm and also to study for this prestigious, globally recognised qualification", says Helen, who has found that being qualified with ACCA has opened many possibilities at Ernst & Young.

"There are so many opportunities available to accountants," Helen says, and the global element of the ACCA Qualification allows her to plan for the future. "It is good to know that working overseas is an option. It also opens up the possibility of short-term secondments to other countries, which is a very exciting prospect."

Ernst & Young has provided Helen with the support and encouragement she needed to gain her ACCA Qualification, and she will never look back. "There are so many interesting roles within the profession and you have the opportunity to meet a wide range of people," Helen remarks.

The ACCA Qualification has enabled Helen to progress her career and continue to develop her technical expertise, as well as offering her a choice of sectors and company sizes. "The hard work you put in will be a benefit in the long term," she concludes.

Chartered Institute of Management Accountants (CIMA)

Management accountants work in organisations of all sizes and in all sectors – 183,000 members in 168 countries. They are well represented in manufacturing and in service industries (only about 1% work in practice, 16% in the public sector, and nearly three quarters are employed in commerce and industry). People often view accountancy in terms of auditing, but management accountants are much more involved with the day-to-day running and decision-making; they are, as the name suggests, focused on management accounting. Management accountants are big picture 'doers', not number-crunching theorists. High street accountants to the public, and those offering business forecasting and planning in larger Public Practices may sometimes also be CIMA-qualified (www.cimaglobal.com).

Whereas financial accountants follow generally accepted accounting practices (GAAP), management accountants select their approaches and techniques from various academic and commercial sources, providing greater freedom and scope for creativity. The CIMA syllabus does not cover audit so CIMA members are not able to work in Public Practice undertaking audits projects, but they can work in advisory and consultancy divisions. CIMA members would need to cross-qualify with ACA or ACCA and this would require several years' practical audit experience plus additional qualifications.

As a CIMA-qualified 'financial business partner', you would analyse costs, profitability and performance, and prepare budgets across the organisation, which would call for a central role in understanding, advising, planning and forecasting on key commercial strategies, and managing risks. You would look to the future and take a predictive rather than retrospective approach (as in auditing). Again, you could face particular pressure at financial year and month ends. Additionally, you may negotiate with corporate financiers and communicate financial information to managers in other functions. You may monitor and evaluate financial information systems and internal controls, and design rewards structures for shareholders and senior executives.

Why choose CIMA? This respected and internationally recognised qualification is specifically tailored for working in business, and you may progress to high-paid, prestigious positions.

CIMA's commercial emphasis is particularly apparent when you look at syllabuses for other professional bodies. Compared with ACCA, CIMA uniquely covers operations, change management, marketing, and relationship and project management, with greater emphasis on HR management and techniques of applied management accounting. ACCA, on the other hand, unlike CIMA, covers taxation, external audit and assurance (CIMA members are not qualified to undertake audit) and law (covered earlier at certificate stage), and focuses differently on information systems.

The CIPFA syllabus, which is, of course, by definition tailored toward the public sector, does not incorporate CIMA's operational management, marketing, business economics and law, or strategic management modules, but it does uniquely cover public sector-specific accounting issues, external audit and taxation, and it places a different emphasis on audit and assurance, and public finance and policy.

CIMA is an internationally recognised qualification and training, again, combining professional examinations and three years' relevant practical experience (gained with an employer who can provide appropriate experience or a formal training scheme – although even university work experience can count). It is sensible to look for good study leave packages, because study when taking such responsibility can be very hard. In consultation, the syllabus is revised every four years to reflect the needs of global business. In addition to the fundamentals of accounting, CIMA covers strategic business and management skills:

- analysis to inform business decisions

- strategy to generate wealth and shareholder value

- risk identification and management

- planning and budgeting

- communication – identification of information needs and dissemination of audience-specific messages.

There are three sections – business management, management accounting and financial management, each with two management-level examinations and one at strategic level. The final T4 (formerly known as TOPCIMA) examination is case-study based and draws on a real-life scenario. To achieve chartered status (ACMA – Associate Chartered Management Accountant), all levels must be passed. There are no time restrictions.

What are the CIMA entry requirements?

CIMA has no formal academic prerequisites and is therefore a qualification open to all (so you can work up from junior accounts clerk). However, exemptions gained through a relevant degree or business experience can speed your progress. A pertinent qualification, such as a degree in accounting, economics, business, finance, law and even science, the OU Certificate in Accounting, or an AAT qualification, may exempt you from the CIMA certificate stage. You might then go straight to the Professional Qualification level; otherwise, the Certificate in Business Accounting must be passed before moving on to the CIMA Professional Qualification.

Again, for graduate entry, most employers do tend to insist on 2.i honours and a high UCAS tariff, plus strong English and mathematics. Some even specify particular degree subjects. CIMA accepts BTEC HNDs, but employers may not be as flexible – you may have greater chance as a diplomate with SMEs (small and medium-sized enterprises).

Relevant work experience, as for ACA and ACCA, will be viewed favourably and is becoming increasingly important in the face of strong competition. It is also possible to work as a management accountant after you have qualified with one of the other professional institutes.

Profile: Hughes & Co Ltd

Small provincial firm or large city centre firm?

Your choice of ultimate career path, whilst training either at university
or as an employee of an accountancy practice, will no doubt fill you with fear and trepidation.

Hughes & Co Ltd, Chartered Certified Accountant and Registered Auditor, are a small
provincial firm based in North East Lancashire.

Formed in 1994, the practice assists a wide range of clients, from SMEs to self employed
plumbers. The practice offers a wide range of services to help clients – from basic
bookkeeping and payroll, through to VAT and HMRC compliance and then to management
support work with monthly accounts, budgets and forecasting.

There is then the statutory work that is undertaken, with audit and financial statement
preparation, thereby assisting directors with their duties with the HMRC iXBRL compliance
work that is now required.

Working for a small firm has many advantages in that the work is extremely varied, clients
are always looking for the best support from a Chartered Accountancy practice, and you
can ultimately feel part of the clients' financial and business success.

The disadvantage can be a lack of exposure to major UK listed companies, but often the
larger the firm the less input you may have in advising how your clients can be successful.

Case study

David Hughes is a Chartered Certified Accountant BA (HONS) FCCA FMAAT; here he recounts his career path.

To train to be a qualified Chartered Accountant – ICAEW, ACCA, CIMA, or CIPFA – is long
and onerous.

The progression of exams proves that you have understood the basics and can answer an
examiners question, but your real training takes place after qualification, when you are
exposed to business problems and how to solve them.

"I trained in a local practice taking my qualifications through correspondence courses – no
university life style for me. The work encompassed accounting for the small sole trader
through to a PLC audit – so I had a great grounding and experienced many business styles.
I then moved on to industry to learn how to be a company cost accountant, financial
controller and then to be a financial director within a UK listed group.

"Then I came back into practice with my own firm and went on to open up my own CIMA and ACCA accountancy training school, offering my knowledge and ability to aspiring local students – so that is where I am today.

"So what did my qualification give me? A route to follow my choice of career – practice – industry and finally a maker of my own destiny and I hope fortune!

"Work hard and you will get the results – never underestimate what you are undertaking – and once qualified the world is really what you make of it!

Other skills needed

"It has been my experience that competency in mathematics, both in numerical manipulations and in understanding its conceptual foundations, enhances a person's ability to handle the more ambiguous and qualitative relationships that dominate our day-to-day financial decision-making."

Alan Greenspan

Employers will be looking for evidence of:

- commercial awareness and understanding of, and interest in, the workings of a business and the (global) economy

- a professional, positive and ambitious outlook

- numeracy, analytical, and technical (IT) skills, lateral thinking and logic

- organisational and time management skills, and calmness under pressure (there is always a deadline looming and one may have lots of balls to juggle, in addition to concurrent working and studying)

- people and communication skills (you liaise with all departments and levels)

- influencing and negotiating skills

- language skills, perhaps

- strength as a team player.

Possible career progression

Finance professionals with a broader business and management understanding are much sought after, especially in the current climate where competitiveness is key. CIMA is an internationally recognised qualification, and you would be valued for your global training and multi-departmental involvement and knowledge. The CIMA qualification affords versatility and adaptability, so you might move up the financial hierarchy, into a specialised business or financial analysis position, or into a more general commercial and managerial role (say, general manager, CEO, operations manager, or IT director). Equally, you could move into consultancy or go self-employed. Approximately 20% of FTSE 100 CEOs are CIMA-qualified.

The working environment

The environment is likely to be dynamic, professional and pressurised, but with an underlying routine and work cycle, intermingled with more bespoke reports and projects. You may have to cope with many interruptions and meetings, and many departments all demanding attention and information simultaneously. You may have to work overtime to meet a deadline, but there should not be too much disruption to personal and social life. The typical working week is 44 hours.

Larger organisations can provide more varied experience, but smaller concerns may enable you to work more closely with key decision-makers. Management accountancy can also provide opportunities for travel with multinationals, and CIMA is a valued qualification abroad. Women are somewhat underrepresented, with a male to female ratio of 65:35, but this is gradually changing.

Typical salaries and benefits

Starting salaries are again dependent on sector, location and organisational size, but tend to range from £23,000 to £26,000. Post-qualification salaries range from £25,000 to £57,000 (averaging £35,000) and at senior level, you might expect to earn £62,000 to £106,000, with 11% of CIMA members on at least £100,000 per year. Bonuses and study packages are commonplace.

Your additional benefits would be similar to those of ACA: pension, private health care, life insurance, gym membership, childcare vouchers, car allowance, optional holiday, and subsidised canteen.

Chartered Institute of Public Finance and Accountancy (CIPFA)

"The great thing about working in the accounting department is that everybody counts!"

Anon

The Chartered Institute of Public Finance and Accountancy (CIPFA) is the only professional UK accountancy body which specialises in the public sector. It has a membership of about 13,300. By definition, CIPFA members are less likely to practise as accountants to the general public, and they tend to work for public sector departments or in firms that specialise in supplying accounting services to central and local authority organisations.

Profile: Westminster Business School

Westminster Business School, located in the heart of London, is one of the largest centres for business and management education in the UK.

The school offers a number of specialist business masters courses, recognised and accredited by a number of professional bodies (AMBA, CIPD, CIM, CMI and ACCA), in the areas of:

- **finance and accountancy**
- **economics**
- **marketing**
- **management**
- **human resource management**
- **business information management**
- **MBA**

The school is also conducting applied research that is relevant to all areas of business, much of which has gained an international reputation. Finally, we have built a reputation for enterprise and knowledge transfer in the London region and work with public and private organisations across the UK.

We are London's leading professionally focused and research-informed business school.

The school is cosmopolitan, with a diverse student population which reflects London's demographic variety, and nearly a third of our full-time students come from outside the UK.

Our staff, too, are drawn from many countries, and every year we welcome visiting scholars and researchers from all over the world. Although we are a school with a strongly international outlook, we also draw on a long tradition of providing part-time courses for Londoners. For nearly 80 years the school has served the needs of busy professionals and business people living or working in the capital, giving our full-time students a unique opportunity to network with the active business community.

Our strong links with London business and government enable us to bring practitioners and headline-makers into the classroom on a regular basis. In turn we help to arrange student placements, internships and mentoring, which give our students an important hands-on experience and involvement with the workplace.

The school has growing research and consultancy strengths in a range of areas, including employment research, financial services and international finance, leadership, and business strategy. We host conferences, workshops, seminars and other events open to the public, and regard the dissemination of new ideas to the outside world as an important part of our function.

For more information please visit www.westminster.ac.uk/wbs or contact us at course-enquiries@westminster.ac.uk.

If you are less attracted to commercial arenas and keen to feel that your work is of direct social benefit, then a position in the public or not-for-profit sector, and CIPFA qualification, could be an obvious choice for you.

The Big Four and other professional practice firms do also have public and voluntary sector specialisms. Public sector employers often offer great flexibility and work-life balance as well. Unfortunately, the economic downturn has hit the public sector hard, and organisations traditionally taking on four trainees may now be recruiting just two; they may be investing, instead, in qualified staff, but they should clearly be keeping one eye on succession planning. Some sectors such as health may offer a choice on which qualification is studied, but CIPFA is the preferred qualification in general.

Chartered public finance accountants ensure efficient collection and use of funds in public and voluntary sector concerns like health service trusts, local authorities, housing associations, police and public utility, educational, charitable, and central government organisations. You can be managing very substantial resources and budgets, but these are often frustratingly limited for purpose, especially in the current climate of cutbacks. Trainees can be rotated around departments to broaden experience in larger concerns. While competition for initial training places is still fierce, subsequent positions are easier to obtain.

Your key tasks would involve financial reporting and control: collating financial data and compiling reports to estimate and review costs and budgets for projects, and monitoring investments, spending and cashflow. You would allocate funds to projects and departments, assessing service effectiveness and improving financial systems. You would further conduct internal audits and present management information to budget holders and board members.

Why train with CIPFA? Obviously, if working in the public sector or public services and utilities, or keen to secure a not-for-profit role, then CIPFA is the most appropriate and relevant qualification, being the only one tailored towards the needs of modern public services. In the current climate, the ability to stretch resources and reduce costs without loss of service is vital. CIPFA are clearly the experts in public finance management, with up-to-date knowledge and understanding of the challenges and opportunities, and key issues, policies, and standards. The syllabus is comprehensive, covering not just technical finance and accounting, but also stakeholder communications, ethics and governance, and management and strategy. The CIPFA qualification also affords flexibility in that you can study at a pace to suit yourself and perhaps your employer.

CIPFA is the only chartered organisation in not just the UK, but also the world, to focus on public finance. CIPFA suggests that 80% of training vacancies tend to be found in the public sector and the remaining 20% tend to be with companies serving the public sector, including the Big Four. The latest POB survey reports 63% of CIPFA's members to be currently employed in the public sector, with 3% in professional practice, and 8% in industry and commerce, including public services and utility companies.

Qualifications take three years and there are three parts: certificate, diploma and final test of professional competence, designed to match experience gained on the job. One advantage is that studies are very specific to the public sector and you might apply your learning immediately. Study is usually by day release (two days per week) with some online options. The public sector tends to be more flexible regarding examinations.

- The certificate (CIPFA affiliate membership) includes examination in financial accounting, management accounting, financial reporting, and financial management systems and techniques.

- The diploma (CIPFA associate membership) covers audit and assurance, leadership and management, decision-making accounting, governance and public policy, financial and performance reporting, public finance, and taxation.

- The final test of professional competence (full CIPFA membership) examines strategic business management and a finance and management case study.

What are the CIPFA entry requirements?

Is a degree required?

While open to graduates in any discipline, 2.i honours are generally sought, and the following subjects may be favoured:

- accounting/finance

- business/management

- economics or mathematics

- government and politics

- public administration.

It can be possible to gain entry with an HND, especially in one of the above subjects, and as with a degree, relevant study may provide exemptions from the certificate level of the CIPFA qualification. This is assessed on a case-by-case basis.

The minimum entry level is less demanding at just two A levels and three GCSEs – all at A–C grade and including English and mathematics at either level.

Other skills needed

- Numeracy

- Spoken and written communication skills

- IT literacy

- Analytical and problem-solving skills

- Self-discipline and organisational skills (not just for work, but to combine demands of study and work)

- Team working

Possible career progression

Obviously, there are a vast number of bodies that aim to balance public service costs funded by donation or taxation, rather than to maximise profit. Your progression often follows a clear hierarchy, but should you be prepared to be mobile and to relocate, it helps.

In local government, you are likely to be appointed to a specific role after qualification and you could expect to take responsibility for the overall financial provision of that service or department within a few years. You would progress through taking responsibility for resources or departments of increasing size.

In the longer term, you could move out to Public Practice, or even into a broader public sector management consultancy. Alternatively, you could eventually move into a senior executive position within an organisation such as chief executive of a local authority, charity or health service trust.

The working environment

Your average working week would be 35 to 40 hours, but late weekdays and even weekend work may be required at times (although it is common in the public sector to then take time off in lieu). This is arguably less pressured and demanding than other accountancy specialisms, but it can still have its stresses at busy times like the end of the financial year. Public sector bodies are very open to part-time work, job sharing and flexible working. There tends to be a fairly even male-to-female balance.

Opportunities may be largely in cities and towns. While office-based, you may be required to travel at times (rarely overseas) and the work involves a lot of meetings and consultation with different agencies, funders and departments. Although improving, the bureaucracy, and relatively slow pace and inefficiency can have its frustrations for some people.

Typical salaries and benefits

Starting salaries are said to range from £23,000 to £50,000, with higher pay in London and with the big accountancy firms. A few years after qualification, you should be earning £32,000 to £65,000, and at senior level £35,000 to £100,000. As a local authority director of finance you would earn more than £110,000, plus benefits.

Pension and car allowances are common, and as for ACA, health insurance, gym membership, share options and bonuses may be part of your package in professional practice.

CIPFA
the people
in public finance

\ sharpen your finance skills

Training and Professional Qualifications from CIPFA

Training with CIPFA, the UK's only professional accountancy body to specialise in public services, will provide you with the skills to make a real difference in the public sector throughout your career.

Our qualifications:

- Equip you with knowledge and technical skills to deliver against the challenges and issues you face.
- Cover a range of topics and are based on the latest business practices, set in a public sector context.
- Reward you with recognised and in-demand skills from employers.
- Are delivered across a range of learning styles, and can be tailored to meet your organisational requirements.

To find out more about training with CIPFA visit our website:
www.cipfa.org.uk or contact a Student Advisor on **020 7543 5656**, or email **students@cipfa.org.uk**

Quoting ref: MA0946A1

Profile: CIPFA

CIPFA The Chartered Institute of Public Finance & Accountancy

Professional qualifications

CIPFA, the Chartered Institute of Public Finance and Accountancy, is the professional body for people in public finance. We have been successfully training accountants, financial managers and auditors for over 100 years.

As the only UK professional accountancy body to specialise in public services, our qualifications are the foundation for a career in public finance.

CIPFA Professional Qualification

CIPFA is more than just a professional qualification – it offers attractive and rewarding career options. What really sets us apart is our commitment to developing members into individuals who make an outstanding contribution to the organisations in which they are employed.

The Qualification has been developed with extensive consultation with employers, members, students and academics to ensure that it is the most robust financial management qualification for today's public services.

How the course is structured

Designed in three stages, CIPFA's Professional Qualification has been developed to dovetail with trainees' work placements and the practical skills they acquire. At each stage successful students can apply for membership and receive designatory letters.

Professional Certificate – The modules at this stage are the building blocks of any career in accountancy or financial management. This level gives you the right grounding for your career.

Professional Diploma – Building upon knowledge gained in the Professional Certificate, the diploma focuses on specific public sector business skills and financial topics. It covers areas such as the whole of government accounts procedure, public sector reporting frameworks and public sector borrowing. Although this level focuses on public sector issues, overall knowledge can easily be transferred into the private sector.

Strategic – This is the last stage in becoming a chartered public accountant. It is the culmination of all the skills learnt throughout the qualification and gives students a more focused strategic financial management overview of running major projects and large complex organisations.

On average, the course takes three years to complete. It is most commonly completed during your employment with a public sector organisation or an employer working with a public sector organisation.

Trainee vacancies

Many public sector employers are currently looking to recruit graduates to study for the CIPFA professional qualification, such as the Audit Commission and Department for Work and Pensions.

There are also many private sector companies training for CIPFA, such as KPMG, PKF, PricewaterhouseCoopers and Grant Thornton.

To see a full list of employers currently taking on trainees please visit **www.cipfa.org.uk/trainee**.

Career prospects

Many of our students find their careers progress extremely quickly. Typically, a CIPFA student can earn over £25,000 as a trainee accountant. As a chartered public finance accountant (CPFA), members can expect to earn £40,000 or more as a senior auditor, and well in excess of £100,000 at director or chief executive level.

To find out more about CIPFA and our qualifications, contact a student advisor on 020 7543 5656 or visit www.cipfa.org.uk/career, quoting reference MA0946A1.

Case study

Studying for the CIPFA Professional Qualification

James Donegan works as a Project Assistant for the Metropolitan Police. He studied Accounting and Financial Management at Loughborough University.

"During my degree I had a year's placement working for Caterpillar (a large international manufacturing company). I gained a lot of experience and could see the importance of the advice and information that the finance staff gave to the business to help them make decisions.

"Currently I am working in a project team within finance. I get to interact with people from all over the organisation and my skills are put to the test daily, giving me an opportunity to test out what I have learnt and also quiz the tutors when I get back to studying! By working in this sector I feel I am playing a key role in helping deliver effective public services and I am giving something back to the community."

Qualifying

"My employer pays for all my course and exam fees but they also give me day release to study the qualification in work time. I chose CIPFA as it was the accountancy body that was most relevant to my career, providing practical learning and with a broad range of topics. CIPFA is the only accountancy body that specialises in public services so it didn't make sense to choose any other qualification."

Other specialist bodies

Association of International Accountants (AIA)

Founded in 1928, the Association of International Accountants (AIA; www.aiaworldwide.com) is a lesser known but creditable professional accountancy body which has promoted the notion of 'international accounting', encouraging trust, clarity and shared standards, and it has a global network of over 7,000 members in 85 countries. There are nearly 1,700 members in the UK, working predominantly in companies and 5% in practice. Many of its members are in top positions, from senior management to director level, and represent some of the most major and successful firms.

Entry qualifications are as for CIPFA – two A levels and three GCSEs – all of A–C grade and in different subjects, including English and mathematics at either level. A National Diploma is also sufficient for registration.

There are three levels of qualification: foundation, certificate (professional level 1) and diploma (professional level 2).

1. Foundation level modules include Financial Accounting 1, Business Economics, Management Accounting 1, Auditing and Taxation, and Information Processing.

2. The Certificate in Accounting (professional level 1) covers Auditing, Company Law, Management Information, Business Management, Financial Accounting 2, and Management Accounting 2.

3. The Diploma in Accounting (professional level 2) examines Financial Accounting 3, Financial Management, Professional Practice (Auditing), Taxation and Tax Planning.

Additionally, qualification requires three years' work experience.

As with ICAEW, ACCA, ICAS and ICAI, the AIA is, since July 1994, a recognised UK qualifying body for statutory auditors, and it oversees its members regarding money laundering. It is currently recognised in over 30 countries. High standards in their professional qualifications are ensured by both internal and external or independent adjudicators.

Like CIMA, this has quite a commercial focus, but unlike CIMA you would, if AIA-qualified, be authorised to undertake audit. With increased globalisation, this qualification may obviously become more popular. However, while four times as many AIA-qualified accountants work abroad as in the UK, they are still in significantly fewer numbers than ACCA-qualified accountants, who have double their UK number working overseas (7,000 AIA and 14,000 ACCA).

Profile: Association of International Accountants (AIA)

THE ASSOCIATION OF INTERNATIONAL ACCOUNTANTS

The Association of International Accountants (AIA) was founded in the UK in 1928 as a professional accountancy body, and from the outset has promoted the concept of 'international accounting,' to create a global network of accountants in over 85 countries worldwide.

CREATING WORLD CLASS ACCOUNTANTS

AIA offers a choice of five accountancy qualifications, including a Certificate in Accountancy, Diploma in Accountancy, Diploma in Professional Accountancy, the AIA Professional Accountancy Qualification and the AIA Statutory Auditor Qualification.

Qualifying with AIA will equip you with the skills you need to succeed in any accountancy and finance role, and at any level. AIA is recognised by the UK government as a recognised qualifying body for statutory auditors under the Companies Act 2006, and also has recognition to operate in the Qualifications and Credit Framework (QCF) as an awarding body. The AIA professional qualification is currently recognised in over 30 countries worldwide.

AIA is committed to creating world-class accountants who have the skills, the knowledge and the ethics to help business grow.

Association of International Accountants
Staithes 3, The Watermark, Metro Riverside, Newcastle upon Tyne, NE11 9SN
T: 0191 493 0277 F: 0191 493 0278
E: aia@aiaworldwide.com W: www.aiaworldwide.com

Case study

Abhik Nag is a trainee accountant and currently a Client Relationship Manager at PKB International Ltd, an international accountancy practice, also based in Bristol, and with a number of European associated offices. It is part of the PKB Group, based in the UK, which has a strong auditing arm.

Abhik graduated from the University of Hertfordshire in 2010, with a degree in Management Science with Economics, and chose to develop his accounting career by taking advantage of the AIA Audit Scholarship scheme.

"The AIA Statutory Auditor Qualification is recognised by the UK government, and will give me the skills required to progress my career. My role within PKB has already changed as a result. I chose to study with AIA because they have offered me excellent guidance and advice, and the audit scholarship is an offer not to be missed!

"AIA has a good reputation, and colleagues recommended it to me on the basis that it would give me a solid foundation from which to build my career. Whilst I am following the audit route, the AIA syllabus is broad-based so I can ultimately choose to work in any area of accountancy.

"In my current role I'm responsible for client relationship matters, working closely with the local partner and his team. This allows me to fully understand the client's needs, and the assurance services required. It helps me to put into context the progressive exposure I am getting on the planning and the practical work required to qualify as a professional accountant and statutory auditor. Working while I am studying will help me to reinforce my theoretical knowledge with practical experience.

"As my career has only just started, I think it's more about how AIA will help me in the future. I think the single biggest benefit of being part of a professional body is that it's essentially a quality standard, so you're recognised as a world-class accountant. I could go and work anywhere in the world, and prospective employers would know I was trained to the very highest standard."

Association of International Accountants
Staithes 3, The Watermark, Metro Riverside, Newcastle upon Tyne, NE11 9SN
T: 0191 493 0277 F: 0191 493 0278
E: aia@aiaworldwide.com W: www.aiaworldwide.com

Chartered Institute of Taxation (CIOT)

Established in 1930, the Chartered Institute of Taxation (www.tax.org.uk) received its Royal Charter in 1994. This (world's largest) professional taxation institute has about 15,000 members.

Chartered tax advisers largely work in dedicated departments in high street accountancy firms and internally in businesses. There are some tax specialist firms, but most offer accountancy and bookkeeping services too. While tax specialists, you may advise on and produce general accounts for small limited companies (other than audit), and rental statements. As a trainee, you may choose the CIOT qualification, or even simultaneously study for ACA and CIOT qualifications, if working in the taxation division.

*"In this world nothing can be said to be certain, except death
and taxes."*

Benjamin Franklin

Institute of Financial Accountants (IFA)

Established in 1916, the Institute of Financial Accountants (www.ifa.org.uk) is
the oldest and largest body of non-Chartered Accountants in the world (non-
Chartered Accountants includes those who are AAT and CAT-qualified, and part-
qualified individuals).

Membership is aimed at those working in commerce with SMEs (small and medium-
sized enterprises), or who work in small and medium-sized accountancy practices
(SMPs) which advise SMEs.

The IFA represents its members and students in over 80 countries and it offers
financial accountant qualifications and continuous professional development.

Association of Corporate Treasurers (ACT)

The ACT (www.treasurers.org) qualifies, supports and represents its members
working in corporate finance, treasury, and risk, and it professes to be the leading
professional body for international treasury, defining standards, promoting best
practice and supporting continuing professional development – the voice of
corporate treasury representing the members' interests. It has members in 87% of
the FTSE 100 companies. There is a fast-track route if you are already a qualified
accountant. While an exciting field, treasury is rarely viewed as the starting point
for new graduates.

As a treasurer, you would be concerned with financial policy and strategy, and with
banking, funding and investments, restructuring and balancing debt, equity, foreign
exchange, cost and risk, and ensuring sufficient liquidity to meet potential demand.
In some organisations, you might also take responsibility for pensions, insurance,
property and taxation.

Bookkeeping bodies

Every company is legally required to keep financial records or 'books', whether manually in ledgers, or entered electronically on computer. Bookkeeping is a growing and international profession, which involves understanding and monitoring the workings of a business through the keeping of accurate figures. Auditors like to know that they have figures they can trust.

As a bookkeeper, you might process data, maintain databases and ledgers, create cashflow forecasts, complete tax returns (self-assessment or VAT) and draft final accounts for sole traders and limited companies, and handle payroll runs.

Should you be an organised, methodical type or perfectionist, who gains satisfaction from documenting and entering data, and seeing a balanced set of accounts, bookkeeping could suit you. You may be a school leaver, a more mature career changer or woman returner, or perhaps even a stay-at-home mother, who wants a small home-based business.

As a bookkeeper you might work for yourself from home, or you might work internally with companies of all sizes, or even in Public Practices, large or small.

Accounting software

It would be sensible to see what software skills appear to be most in demand in the kind of firms that most appeal to you.

Many bookkeeping courses teach the use of popular accounting software, such as Sage, Quickbooks, software from Microsoft, or web-based providers like Intacct and NetSuite.

Proficiency and experience with the most popular packages may add weight to your CV.

Some bookkeeping courses are partnered with accounting software provider Sage, where you have the opportunity to train with the software and therefore get a thorough knowledge of it.

International Association of Book-keepers (IAB)

Founded in 1973, the IAB used to focus solely on supporting professionalism and qualification in bookkeeping. In recent years, IAB have expanded their offerings to provide essential financial and business skills, also appropriate for budding entrepreneurs wishing to start or develop a small business (few new businesses actually survive the first two years, often due to poor planning and financial awareness).

Like AAT and CAT, IAB qualifications are respected, standalone awards, but you can also use them as a stepping stone towards other professional qualifications. The IAB qualifications can provide eligibility for exemptions from elements of the main professional bodies' examinations: ICAEW, ACCA, CIMA, CIPFA, IFA, AAT and IPP (Institute of Payroll Professionals).

The IAB has partnered with accounting software provider Sage to offer a Computerised Accounting for Business qualification (level 1, 2 or 3), which provides additional endorsement and certification by Sage, so you can be both IAB and Sage-qualified through the one course.

Do you wish to further develop your bookkeeping and accounting skills?

There is no better way to study for and achieve an **IAB** qualification

IAB
Qualifications for business

- Designed by practising, professional industry experts providing technical skills needed by businesses and other organisations
- Accredited qualifications - regulated by Ofqual (the Office of the Qualifications and Examinations Regulator in England)
- Examinations which lead to qualification and membership of a professional body, including the International Association of Accounting Professionals (IAAP) and the International Association of Book-keepers (IAB)

- Known globally, with members and students in more than 60 countries
- Range of short as well as larger, 'full' or 'competence' qualifications, building skills in bite-size chunks
- Accepted for entry to, or partial exemption from, UK university programmes & recognised by UK Chartered Accountancy bodies – ICAEW, ACCA, CIMA and CIPFA

Study with the valuable support of an IAB Accredited Centre (by attending a course or by distance learning).

For further details please visit **www.iabq4b.org**

International Association of Book-keepers
Suite 30, 40 Churchill Square, Kings Hill, West Malling, Kent, ME19 4YU
Tel: 0844 330 3527 (UK Only)
E-mail: **mail@iab.org.uk**
Company Registration No 1119378 (England)
Limited (by guarantee)

Profile: the IAB

What is the IAB?

A leading professional and awarding body . . .

The International Association of Book-keepers (IAB) was founded in 1973 and until approximately ten years ago it focussed purely on being a professional and examining body for bookkeepers. Building on this, today the IAB is the leading UK and international professional body for those providing bookkeeping and related accounting services to small businesses. Through its broad range of Ofqual-accredited qualifications and its CPD activities, the IAB aims to meet the extensive financial skills needs of young people and adults and to provide essential business skills for those starting or developing a small business.

International . . .

Interest in the IAB is ever increasing and it continues to grow both in the UK and internationally, with members and students now in five figures and spread across approximately 60 countries.

An approved supervisory body . . .

The IAB is an approved supervisory body under the UK Money Laundering Regulations 2007 – an important role, meaning that those IAB members who are registered with the Association as being 'in practice' are supervised and also are not required to separately register to be supervised by HM Revenue & Customs in compliance with the regulations.

A committed collaborative partner . . .

The IAB has a significant involvement with, and is a willing partner of, national government and standard-setting bodies.These include the HMRC Employment Consultation Forum, Financial Services Authority (FSA), Qualifications and Curriculum Authority/Ofqual, Financial Skills Partnership (FSP) and the Small Firms Enterprise Development Initiative (SFEDI).

In 2010 and 2011, working with the FSP and other awarding bodies, the IAB has taken the lead role in developing bookkeeping units for the new Qualifications and Credit Framework (QCF) in England, Wales and Northern Ireland and has worked very closely with the IPP in the development of QCF payroll units. In addition, working with the Financial Skills Partnership (FSP) and other awarding bodies, the IAB has played a leading role in creating apprenticeships in bookkeeping and a revised payroll apprenticeship.

An awarding body of recognised qualifications . . .

The current range of IAB qualifications now numbers more than 20. In addition to the IAB's 'core' qualifications in bookkeeping, accounting and payroll, the range now includes Finance for Non-Financial Managers, Small Business Financial Management, Business Enterprise and Business Law. In 2008, the levels were expanded so that the IAB now offers 'foundation' level qualifications at NQF level 1 through levels 2 and 3 to level 4. Several of these qualifications have been granted exemptions by the UK chartered accountancy bodies – ICAEW, ACCA,

CIMA and CIPFA. The effect of this is to extend the skills of learners and also to provide complete progression routes from level 1 through to level 4 and on to a range of financial careers including registered bookkeeper, Chartered Accountant and payroll professional.

Simple steps to becoming a qualified professional bookkeeper

Step 1
Become a student member of the IAB by studying for an IAB professional qualification – safe in the knowledge that IAB qualifications, accredited by Ofqual, are further underpinned by the recognition of chartered accountancy bodies such as ACCA, CIMA, ICAEW and CIPFA. To find an IAB Accredited Centre (including distance learning) to help you achieve, visit **www.iabq4b.org.**

Step 2
Having achieved your IAB (or comparable) qualification, you can immediately apply for employment or use your skills in your own business or organisation. In summary, by achieving an IAB qualification at the following levels, in either or both manual and computerised bookkeeping/accounting, you have demonstrated that you can:

- **Level 1:** enter transactions into bookkeeping records/system

- **Level 2:** maintain records and prepare a trial balance

- **Level 3:** make complex bookkeeping adjustments and reconciliations and prepare financial statements for sole traders, partnerships and not-for-profit organisations

- **Level 4:** prepare financial statements for limited companies.

Step 3
Once qualified at level 2 or above, you should immediately apply to become a full member of the IAB. This will demonstrate to others your ongoing commitment to maintain and enhance your professionalism. It also gives you access to an extensive range of member benefits, including regular technical updates and member seminars to assist you to keep up to date with, for example, HMRC and other developments.

Step 4 (Just for those setting up in business as a bookkeeper)
Importantly, should you wish to open your own bookkeeping practice (to offer bookkeeping or accounting services to clients), as an IAB member you will be eligible to apply for an additional certificate enabling you to be supervised by the IAB. Registration to be supervised is a statutory requirement under the Money Laundering Regulations 2007, failure to do so being a criminal offence. The IAB provides access to an *IAB Members' Handbook* on its website. This is a **valuable resource for members**, particularly those in practice, containing useful information and guidance as well as template documents that members may choose to adapt for their own use in practice. If you are considering setting up in practice, below is an additional quick guide to what you may need to consider.

Checklist for starting your own bookkeeping business

- Obtaining your qualification and becoming a supervised IAB member to comply with the money laundering regulations

- Deciding where you are going to work (home, office or premises of clients)

- Obtaining an appropriately specified computer and software

- Promotion – networking, mailshots, advertising

- Professional indemnity insurance

- Deciding how much you are going to charge

- Letter of engagement and anti-money laundering procedures

- Registering under data protection requirements

- Continuing with your professional development and keeping up to date.

Editorial: Golding Computer Services

The new IAB Computerised Accounting for Business
Career path to a rewarding business career . . .

golding computer services

The new International Association of Book-keepers **Computerised Accounting for Business** QCF Accredited Qualifications provide all the theoretical and practical Sage accounts skills employers value so highly.

Uniquely, the Sage provided and IAB approved, course resources provided by Golding Computer Services for each qualification, includes a copy of the Sage 50 Accounts Professional program, to be used for the duration of the training, together with Skills and Knowledge Workbooks.

Designed to provide a thorough working knowledge of computerised accounting, at the appropriate level, the courses also provide a comprehensive understanding of the concepts and legislative background required by a bookkeeper working in a business environment. On successful completion of the level 2 qualification candidates can apply for Associate Membership of the International Association of Book-keepers, with higher levels of membership at Level 3.

By providing entry at Levels 1 and 2, and with no specific educational or experience requirements, the range of qualifications is an ideal starting point for anyone looking for a career in bookkeeping and accounts.

With a background of 29 years' experience as an on-the-job Sage training provider, Golding Computer Services, working closely with Sage and the IAB, has developed *On the Job* Distance Learning Courses which can be undertaken either at home or in the workplace.

By giving the chance to study at home or in the workplace the courses provide the opportunity for someone who may have left the education system with few qualifications to gain accredited qualifications while undertaking their daily duties. Successful completion of Level 3 can provide the possible progression to a degree in computerised accounting that can be achieved whilst working.

Qualifications overview:
IAB Level 1 Award in Computerised Accounting for Business (QCF – 6 Credits)

Starting with the basic routines relating to the entry of bookkeeping transactions into a computerised accounting system.

IAB Level 2 Certificate in Computerised Accounting for Business (QCF – 13 Credits)

Manual and Computerised accounting principles are brought together so the learner can process and understand the primary transactions within a business.

IAB Level 3 Certificate in Computerised Accounting for Business (QCF – 20 Credits)

This qualification incorporates management reporting and financial statements and covers fixed assets, stock and doubtful debts. On line reporting for VAT is included as well as cash management, and different types of business organisations. A prior knowledge of computerised accounts and double entry bookkeeping to Level 2 standard would be required before starting to study at this level.

If you wish to find out more about these courses and other IAB and Sage Bookkeeping and Payroll courses, or Book-keeping Apprenticeships, please contact training@goldings.info

Institute of Certified Bookkeepers (ICB)

The Institute of Certified Bookkeepers awards qualifications based on academic attainment and experience and provides ongoing, free technical support to members. It further promotes bookkeeping as a profession, ensuring that standards are upheld.

The institute promotes training in bookkeeping, both as a means of increasing competence and confidence, but also to boost career prospects and as a stepping stone to higher level financial qualifications (although the AAT does not award exemptions for the ICB qualification).

Training providers commonly offer training courses in both bookkeeping and Sage, but the Institute of Certified Bookkeepers has partnered with Sage and the Home Learning College to provide a dual distance learning course training for both the ICB Level 11 Certificate and the Sage Certificate of Competency. You might sit the paper at home and this will be followed up with a telephone interview from the ICB.

MAKING YOU COUNT

**THE INSTITUTE
OF CERTIFIED
BOOKKEEPERS**

SUCCESS you can count on

"My qualification gave me the
independence and courage
to run my own business"
Rebecca Ray MICB CB.Cert

The route to your successful bookkeeping career
0845 060 2345 www.bookkeepers.org.uk www.facebook.com/ICBUK @ICBUK

Profile: Institute of Certified Bookkeepers

THE INSTITUTE
OF CERTIFIED
BOOKKEEPERS

What is bookkeeping?

Bookkeeping is the new accounting. That's the message from the world's leading institute for bookkeepers, the Institute of Certified Bookkeepers (ICB).

For many years, people who wanted to get into a worthwhile career in the finance sector have thought that accounting was the only route to success. Not so any more. A career as a bookkeeper may well suit your lifestyle better. And for those who still want to be accountants, but want to prove to prospective employers that they have a broad understanding of what they do, bookkeeping provides the underpinning knowledge that is the foundation of the whole accounting structure.

So what's the difference between an accountant and a bookkeeper?

Accounting remains a brilliant career for those people capable of achieving an excellent degree who want to go on to rule the world. But many have more realistic aspirations and want a career that allows them to really get under the skin of the business for which they work; to become an indispensable part of it. They want to have a closer, more regular business relationship, rather than just at year end or when the proprietors are seeking to sell their business.

More firms of accountants now actively seek people with the broader skills achieved through the more in-depth bookkeeping training. This is particularly the case for accounting firms that deal with smaller companies or insolvency, where a good bookkeeper is needed to go into a company and really understand what the company is doing and where it can make improvements.

Bookkeeping also opens up the prospect of self-employment. Self-employed or freelance bookkeepers are in huge demand right across the country. Why? Because 90% of UK businesses are classed as 'micro' or 'small', so the number of businesses out there that need to keep proper financial records is absolutely huge – around four million.

Many small businesses keep their own books but this often leads to delays in preparing the accounts, which in turn can lead to penalties. Business owners are just too busy running the business to have enough time to do the books and, more often than not, they have neither the skill nor the inclination to give them the attention they deserve. Up steps the bookkeeper.

The Institute of Certified Bookkeepers

Victoria House
64 Paul Street
London
EC2A 4NG
0845 060 2345
www.bookkeepers.org.uk
info@bookkeepers.org.uk
We look forward to helping you succeed

You and the Institute of Certified Bookkeepers

The Institute of Certified Bookkeepers (ICB) was established to provide a series of professional qualifications that reflect the needs of business and the aspirations of people wanting to enter the profession. It exists to represent bookkeepers at all levels and to promote the professionalism of bookkeepers to business, government and the general public.

The ICB has in excess of 150,000 students and members across more than 50 countries, making it the largest bookkeeping institute in the world.

Bookkeeping is an important profession – it is demanding, exciting, challenging and, above all, rewarding.

Bookkeeping provides outstanding career opportunities for men and women of all ages and backgrounds.

Whether you want to work in an accounts department, want to start your own bookkeeping business, or simply want to look after the books of your own or your partner's business, success as a bookkeeper can be yours.

"The great advantage of the ICB qualification is that it lends itself to so many subsequent areas; you could keep going in a bookkeeping route, go into taxation, or you could go into industry. It's both a destination in itself and an opportunity for people to develop their careers beyond it."

Angus Farr, Moore Stephens Chartered Accountants

"It's so easy, once you're in there and you've got the confidence, your business will grow just by word of mouth."

Suzanne Kaufman, Freelance Certified Bookkeeper

"The ICB qualification helped me get the job, and the ICB technical support line gives me the confidence to do the job."

Wendy Shallcroft, Employed Certified Bookkeeper

Association of Accounting Technicians (AAT) bookkeeping course

The AAT is discussed in detail in chapter 5. AAT runs the ABC Bookkeeping qualification, which provides exemption from its foundation level AAT qualification. However, it is noteworthy that the Open University course B190 is actually said to be the same as the ABC one, yet it provides eligibility for more exemptions.

3

Choosing the right path

Making the right choice for you

Everyone should have a clear career direction and an action plan, and while your personal circumstances, motivations and personality will change over the years and contribute to your seeking different things from work at different times as you change, develop and grow, it is sensible to know where you want to head, and why, at least in the short to medium term.

Obviously, there will be some scope to switch roles, organisations, specialisms and sectors, whichever professional qualification you choose, but the different accountancy routes and qualifications can have a different emphasis, thus preparing you better for certain roles and career paths than for others, both in terms of practical skills and in terms of marketability. It is important to understand the differences.

It helps to view your career as a journey. The *Oxford English Dictionary* defines 'career' as a person's 'course or progress through life (or a distinct portion of life)'. This provides a greater sense of fluidity and forward thrust, and it negates the feeling that you should be sitting on the fence while looking for the perfect round hole for your particular round peg. That said, you do need to start with thorough self-assessment, to try to identify whether ACA, CIMA, ACCA or CIPFA would best meet your requirements and which sector or type of organisation would best play to your current motivations, values and personal qualities. Try to be objective and honest about yourself, considering weaknesses and development needs in addition to strengths.

Choosing your qualification

Questions to ask yourself

In order to help you decide which accounting path is right for you, consider the below questions, and try to marry your answers up with what you know about the different qualifications.

- Would you envisage yourself as an external adviser or business partner, working in *professional practice* and providing services to client companies, or would you rather be in an *internal* team, working together to ensure the commercial success of the business?

- Are you the *analytical* auditor or financial analyst, or the more *lateral thinking* corporate financier or management accountant? Are you retrospective or forward thinking?

- Would you prefer to make best use of *public funds*, or would you prefer to maximise profit for a *commercial* firm?

- Are you prepared to work *long hours* and to *travel* extensively for lengthy periods, or do you want a more *balanced* lifestyle?

- Would you prefer to be *quietly problem-solving*, checking and investigating, or do you see yourself having *lots of meetings* and dealing with people?

- Do you want to be *fire-fighting* and trying to turn a company around, or would you value more routine *maintenance*?

- Do you relish a fast-paced *corporate arena* or would you fit more comfortably into a smaller, more friendly and *personal setting*, where you might be a bigger fish in a smaller pond?

- Are you more excited by the idea of *advising individuals* or *big corporations*?

- Do you want to be a *generalist* or a *specialist*?

- Are you considering a certain role to please someone else, because *that is what people from your background do*, or because you cannot think of anything else, or are you considering it to really *suit who you are* and capitalise on what you represent as a human resource?

- Are you chasing the *money* or the *job*?

- Are you happy to be tied to the *same firm* while you train, or do you want to be able to *change jobs* as you please?

Key differences in qualifications

We discussed the main differences in the qualifications in chapter 2. But to briefly remind you:

- ICAEW and ACA may have greater prestige and more of a technical slant, but they are the qualifications of choice for the majority in the major accountancy practices

- ACCA provides similar versatility, but is a more globally recognised qualification, and you are not committed to working for the same employer while studying

- CIMA is more broadly commercially focused and more strategic and forward-looking, but you are not qualified to work in external audit

- CIPFA is specifically designed for working in the public sector and for maximising public funds and investments.

Obviously, the nature of the work will vary greatly not only according to the qualification but also depending on the role or specialism you ultimately choose. If you are innovative and strategic, you may be more drawn to CIMA, or to a future position as a financial director or CEO. If you are very organised and efficiency-conscious, you may favour ACCA for its performance improvement modules and envisage a future career in financial control, systems or operations management.

If you enjoy detailed technical analysis and investigation, you may be particularly attracted to ACA and your dream career might be as an audit partner or forensic specialist.

Then again, should you particularly enjoy researching and writing reports, you may see yourself as a financial accountant, and should you really enjoy project work, digging into the detail and finding solutions, financial analysis may hold particular appeal.

A 'big picture' person may favour management accountancy to auditing, or may prefer to work in a smaller practice where you may be more of a generalist, advising SMEs. On the other hand, a person who is less 'black or white' and stronger verbally may be drawn to the legislative and interpretive aspects of taxation. Someone more sensitive, altruistic, and socially and politically minded, might see CIPFA as the only option, or may choose to transfer in-house with a not-for-profit concern after qualification. Whichever route you take, there is a role, specialism or sector to match who you are and who you may become in the longer term.

While pay, scope for promotion and level of responsibility may be drivers and motivators in early years (with range of work and opportunities for training and development being quite important as well), with seniority, accountants' priorities are more likely to be range of work, level of responsibility, and cultural climate, with pay being further down the list. That said, a recent CIPD Employee Outlook survey found that 'increased pay and benefits' (54%) had just nudged above 'improved job satisfaction' as the primary motivator for a job change, no doubt due to the current economic climate and people feeling the pinch.

Profile: London School of Accountancy and Management

London School of Accountancy and Management (LondonSAM) is a popular professional accountancy college located in the City of London and has a thriving student population ever since it first opened its doors early in the new millennium. The school offers a range of programmes and professional certifications as well as academic degrees, for aspiring accountants, in a variety of formats.

The professional courses at LondonSAM are highly popular as they combine approved study material, experienced tutors, online and offline support, mock tests, regular feedback, question-based revision and special exam techniques courses. LondonSAM's teaching team consists of a number of well-known tutors, including Tony Surridge, Colin Channer, Rob Moulin and Chris Cane, among others.

With most accountants based in the City of London, LondonSAM is the gateway for aspiring accountants to get their chartered qualifications. LondonSAM works with the two main chartered accountancy bodies and is a 'gold' tuition provider for the Association of Chartered Certified Accountants (ACCA) and a Chartered Institute of Management Accountants (CIMA) quality learning partner.

The range of courses at LondonSAM will suit working professionals within the Square Mile. Its students come from a wide range of industries and companies such as Estée Lauder, IBM (UK), Le Meridian Piccadilly, Brokerage City Link, Insight Investment, Lambert Smith Hampton, J C Decaux, HM Treasury, the Bank of England, University College London, City of London Council, Great Ormond Street Hospital and so on.

LondonSAM has produced students who have excelled in professional examinations. One came out fourth worldwide in CIMA examinations and another stood eighth worldwide in two of the subjects.

Apart from the professional courses, LondonSAM offers a range of academic programmes for aspiring accountants, including BSc in Applied Accounting from Oxford Brookes University, credit transfer options to MBA programmes offered by the University of Wales and Staffordshire University, and a top-up BA programme in Accounting and Finance for students with a Higher Diploma in a related area. For practising accountants, there is an option of a part-time MBA, taught one evening a week over three years.

With its 38,000-square-foot campus next to London Guildhall, within walking distance of 16 underground and mainline train stations, LondonSAM is an exciting location for a budding accountant to be.

Case study

Getting into accountancy may lead to a rewarding career, but the path to this is always fraught with challenges. This is about not just meeting the extremely high standards that the British Professional Bodies set for any aspiring accountant, but also gaining the other softer skills, confidence, communication and ability to present oneself well, and developing a rounded professionalism without which it is difficult to attain professional success even after gaining the necessary certification.

Juan Ma, who studied for and successfully attained CIMA certification at the London School of Accountancy and Management (LondonSAM), explains: "It is not just about knowing the subjects, but also about being able to handle the examination questions in the manner expected by the examiners, knowing the right words to use, managing the time effectively and being confident about my own abilities all the time.

"And after you get your certificate, that's just the beginning rather than the end. There starts your search for a professional career, which will require great communication skills, the ability to carry yourself in presentations, proving yourself to be ethical and competent. Being an accountant is not just knowing the accounting principles, but being a complete professional whose key skill happens to be in accounting."

Paul Brewster, who completed ACCA in LondonSAM and then went on to complete an MBA taking advantage of credit waiver and chose to become an educationalist, talks about seeing it from the other side of the fence. He recalls his student days when he would be anxious to know the magic formula, the right answers, to pass the examination. But as he went through the process of qualifying and turning himself into a professional, he seemed to discover there is more to being a successful accountant than just knowing accounting.

He elaborates: "It is about discovering that the rules of professional life, the process of reflection and continuous improvement, the feeling of responsibility towards the clients, and now to my students, and setting a standard of behaviour and meeting that standard every time."

Dr Dak Patel, the Principal of LondonSAM, has seen many students go through the transformation from 'being a student' to 'being a professional', and believes it needs more than just teaching to make the journey. He has set up 'incubation' communities of aspiring young accountants, those who have not got started yet, which helps the candidates in their journey from being students to being professionals.

Available free online through the twin community sites, www.thinkacca.me and www.thinkcima.me.

Case study

Pauline Wallace is UK Head of Public Policy and Regulatory Affairs at PwC.

"What can I do with a modern languages degree that doesn't involve teaching or translating?" This was the question I posed when I met my university's careers guidance counsellor for the first time back in the mid-seventies. For her, the answer was clear – either accountancy or banking, both of which were actively seeking graduates with non-specialist degrees.

As I looked at the options, chartered accountancy had clear attractions. The large firms (there were eight major players and a number of sizeable mid-tier firms at the time) all offered three-year training contracts designed to develop practical skills at the same time as preparing students for the daunting professional exams. For those who were successful (and, at its toughest, the pass rate in the final professional exams was only 19%!), the way was open to move into business, finance, education, the public sector or, indeed, to stay in the profession. Banking in those days seemed to offer a much more limited career track, so I joined a mid-tier firm and trained as an auditor.

Life as an auditor in the mid-seventies was very different than it is today. For the technology- savvy youth of today, it will be hard to imagine, but computerised audit was an obscure back-office role that operated in isolation from the rest of the audit team.

Audit files contained reams of 7-, 14- and even 21-column analysis paper documenting in pencil the results of detailed substantive tests with a series of complicated tick marks as audit trail.

There were relatively few accounting standards and even fewer auditing ones, and there was no external inspection of our work. But the core principles that underpin an audit today – understanding the business, challenging management, using judgement and exercising scepticism – were recognisable then too.

Once qualified, the world opened up and I left my mid-tier firm to explore what else was out there. My initial plans to use my qualification as a springboard to move into business never came to fruition, but that is not necessarily a bad thing. My career has been a source of great enjoyment for me.

A short period as an auditor in Germany was followed by six years in Hong Kong where, amongst other things, I spent some time as a fraud investigator and wrote a textbook on Hong Kong company law.

A fascination with accounting standards led me into a role as an accounting technical partner, firstly at Arthur Andersen and then, after its demise, at PwC where I spent seven exciting years travelling the world as leader of their global financial instruments accounting team.

This culminated with the financial crisis when accounting for financial instruments literally became front page news and even my mother began to understand the job I do!

My current role, leading PwC's UK public policy team, could not be more different from my start in the profession. Following the financial crisis, the auditing profession has been subjected to investigation by regulators and politicians and we are facing proposals that could have a fundamental impact on the shape of the profession. So my time is occupied developing our responses to proposals, talking to regulators and politicians, and keeping my partners informed of what is happening. But the skills I use today are those I have learned throughout my professional life: communicating with people from a range of backgrounds, understanding the story behind the words, listening to different points of view, building consensus, and challenging conclusions.

When I joined the profession, a senior partner told me that, jokes about dull accountants aside, this was a profession for 'people who like people'. And that is as true today as it was then. And my careers advisor was right too: the qualification was just the starting point that opened up a huge range of opportunities. It was the right choice for me.

Longer-term goals

It is not a case of get into accountancy, qualify and live happily ever after. So many people feel lost without a goal on which to focus: A levels, degree, traineeship, qualification, then what?

While you will not want to plan out and fix in stone your whole working life, you should at least consider all options and permutations. What could be the next step... and the step after that? Career development plans need to be continuously re-evaluated and modified.

What skills and competencies will need to be gained for the next stage? What courses are on offer which will help to future-proof your career? What experience should you be trying to gain? What projects would add weight to a CV? Remember you could move sideways as well as upwards – you may not want additional responsibility or a leadership position. Keep up to date with what is happening in the field, and network... it can still be very much 'who you know, not what you know' beyond that initial graduate assessment centre.

Know your own strengths, weaknesses and market value. Do not expect busy people to simply notice what you do. Humbly, quietly and casually point out what you have achieved or done beyond the call of duty, and volunteer for different or more complex tasks, or bespoke projects.

It can help to consider what your ultimate dream would be. Do you envisage yourself as a partner in professional practice? Would you rather be the CEO of a blue chip? Would you prefer to oversee government or charitable funds, and head up the finance department of a local authority? The diagram on p124 shows some common career paths, but this also demonstrates the possible movement between sectors. Chapter 9 discusses post-qualification options in somewhat greater depth.

At CAMS we don't just prepare you for exams - we prepare you for a career.

Courses offered at CAMS are designed to reflect the realities of the modern changing business environment. We will help prepare you for what can be a lucrative career in accounting, finance and business management and will ensure that you are more attractive to prospective employers.

We offer:

◆ ACCA and the ACCA Oxford Brookes BSc in Applied Accounting
◆ accounting degrees accredited by the internationally renowned University of London – lead by the highly respected Royal Holloway college
◆ first class lecturers with top academic and industry experience
◆ comfortable modern facilities
◆ affordable options in a London location
◆ your best chance of exam success

Contact us today to find out how we can help you to achieve your career ambitions.

info@camscollege.org.uk
0208 848 4447
www.camscollege.org

C | A | M | S
COLLEGE OF ACCOUNTANCY
& MANAGEMENT STUDIES

We look forward to welcoming you to the CAMS community.

Profile: CAMS

The College of Accountancy and Management Studies (CAMS) mission is to provide world-class higher education to students from within and beyond our borders.

CAMS provides a platform for developing excellent people, who are taught to think and act progressively to achieve their goals.

At CAMS we consider our students' academic success and social well-being as a top priority. We offer several highly respected degree programmes and internationally recognised courses, including ACCA, which reflect the realities of the modern changing business environment. Students leave us with a qualification that will elevate their professional standing worldwide.

The college has a very spacious, modern campus in the heart of west London. Our lectures are conducted in large, bright classrooms where our expert tutors use the latest smartboard technology, linked to the college computer network, to provide an interactive and lively classroom environment.

CAMS is a British Accreditation Council-approved college and has been awarded an A rating by the UK Border Agency (UKBA). The college can be found on the UKBA's tier 4 register of sponsors licensed under the points-based system.

To find out more visit: www.camscollege.org or contact us on +44 (0)20 8848 4447 or info@camscollege.org.uk

We prepare you for a career.

Case study

Tamara Ciutac came to the College of Accountancy and Management Studies (CAMS) having achieved a degree in Marketing and the Economy and spent four years studying for her professional ACCA qualification and the ACCA Oxford Brookes BSc degree in Applied Accounting.

Of her time at CAMS, Tamara says:

"Even through the early years, the college did not compromise on the quality of teaching. Lecturers are recruited for their knowledge and teaching ability and have excellent academic and industry experience. CAMS facilities are first class and the materials provided have been current and relevant. The best thing about the college is the environment which encourages you to reach for the stars. All the lecturers and staff are always looking at ways to support our learning and help us in trying to achieve our goals."

Tamara explains that studying for a professional accountancy qualification is not always easy, but that the tremendous benefits definitely make it worthwhile:

"To achieve success you must have the discipline to stick to study routines and to cope with the outside distractions like work, home and family. You need the ability to juggle a lot of balls. But the benefits are that I can now fully appreciate and relate to the functions of my department and how a set of figures reflect on future policy changes.

"Studying for the ACCA Oxford Brookes degree was challenging, but interesting at the same time. You need to apply your acquired knowledge to real situations. I would recommend doing it as, together with the ACCA qualification, it has increased my career prospects and demonstrates key skills and commitment to employers."

And her future plans now that she has qualified?

"I have recently started work as an assistant accountant. I first need to achieve my 36 months' experience in accountancy in order to become a full ACCA member, and then I am considering an MBA."

To find out more visit www.camscollege.org or contact us on +44 (0)20 8848 4447 or info@camscollege.org.uk

We prepare you for a career.

Most common career paths

There are, of course, some well-travelled career paths in accountancy. The diagram on p124 shows you some common routes. It may help you to have a look at the ultimate goal, and work your way back to see what you would need to do to achieve this.

Figure 2: Qualification routes

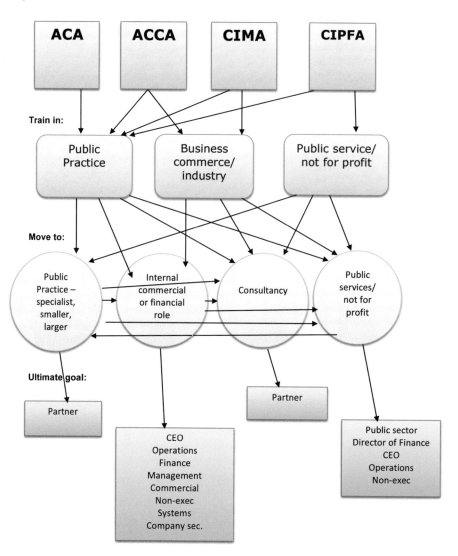

A choice of innovative courses to suit your style of Online Learning.

Kaplan Learn Online courses are expertly designed to prepare you for your career in accounting.

Online
Self study at your own pace

If you are organised and prefer the freedom of self-study in your own time, at your own pace.

- ✓ Access to online tutor debriefs
- ✓ Tutor support in and out of business hours
- ✓ Exam focused study materials†
- ✓ Extensive question practice
- ✓ Online community support, Kaplan Interact

Live Online
The classroom anywhere

If you prefer a structured online experience with the interactivity of the live classroom.

- ✓ The only 100% live classroom experience online with fully interactive lectures
- ✓ Live Support from two expert tutors
- ✓ Facility to playback lectures
- ✓ Exam focused study materials
- ✓ Your own Live Online community.

Kaplan online courses. *Learning experiences as individual as you are.*

* For accountancy courses, as of Jan 2011.
† iPaper version only.

Profile: Kaplan

Over the last 70 years Kaplan has become one of the world's largest providers of diversified education, helping people like you achieve your goals and realise your potential. We have over 30,000 employees in over 30 countries, delivering courses to more than 1 million students annually.

We offer a comprehensive portfolio of market-leading training courses for professional accountancy and tax qualifications, which develop your industry knowledge and technical expertise as well as the key personal and leadership skills required within business.

Kaplan Financial has the combination of award-winning expert tutors, training courses and dedicated support staff to ensure your exam success. Our courses include ACCA, CIMA, AAT and ACA (ICAEW) and are offered in a variety of locations throughout the UK as well as home study options and online learning. So whether you are a school leaver or a university graduate, we can help you realise your potential.

Contact us to find out more about our range of courses today.

BUILDING FUTURES ONE SUCCESS STORY AT A TIME

Case study

Kelly-jayne Johnson

"Due to Kaplan's expertise, professionalism and excellent tuition, I have and will continue to recommend them to other students."

Kelly-jayne Johnson is a Kaplan student who won the 'first in world' prize for the CIMA Financial Strategy paper.*

After graduating from Sheffield Hallam University in Accounting and Financial Management, she knew that she wanted to work in a finance role. She chose Kaplan as a study provider through recommendations from colleagues and never looked back.

Here at Kaplan we understand that everyone is individual and hence so is their learning style. That is why our tutors don't teach from textbooks but bring the lesson to life through real-life examples. They are also there for students right up until they sit their exams – in and out of office hours.

Kelly-jayne cites her Kaplan tutor and the flexibility of ways to study as the key factors in her success.

"My tutor is fantastic, very insightful with real world examples, making learning much more than purely a textbook exercise. The books are incredibly easy to read and provide valuable worked examples and plenty of questions, which definitely aided my learning and revision."

Kaplan's courses are exam-focused to ensure that students pass first time and equip you with the skills that you need to progress your career.

"Undoubtedly my qualification will benefit myself and employer. It has provided me with the academic tools necessary to undertake my role. But, more significantly, it has shaped the way in which I think to a much more professional level than I had previously. The analytical skills that are required to get through the qualification are excellent in helping me provide a valuable role for my employer, but the skills are transferable to many decisions that are made externally from my place of work."

BUILDING FUTURES ONE SUCCESS STORY AT A TIME

* Based on November 2010 exam sitting

Where you work

Type of firm

The nature of the work will vary greatly according to the firm in which you find employment. Not only will the roles and duties be different, but the culture or ethos may be very different too. Therefore, it's a good idea to consider what type of firm you would like to work in from the outset.

Generally, graduate training schemes in Public Practice and blue chip[1] organisations are relatively better paid, and you would join a cohort of the brightest, most confident and most driven young people. This can be fun, dynamic and exciting,

1. Their nickname no doubt stemming from the relatively high value of blue chips in poker, blue chips are high value, reliable stocks, which consistently maintain strong performance on the stock market, irrespective of economic climate. Competition for graduate training in blue chip organisations like Unilever, Mars, WPP, Cargill and Procter & Gamble is as fierce as for the big accountancy firms.

but also hard work and pressurised; some people thrive, whereas others feel that they do not sit comfortably in this aggressive, competitive, materially minded arena. Some firms will not countenance examination failure, which adds to the pressure (find out where you stand with this before you start).

Working in industry or commerce, there may be less travel, and you may be the only trainee in the finance department, which may mean that you have no peers with whom to compare notes. This could equally be the case in a smaller professional practice, but you may feel more supported and valued than in a large corporation.

> *"I am pleased to say that our results are very much in line with plan. All we have to do now is find out what the plan was."*
>
> CFO – *anon for obvious reasons*

Get to know the company

In an article in the *Financial Times* in January 2011, the lead graduate recruitment partner at Deloitte was talking about what both the company and the graduates were looking for in the selection process and choice of firm. He made an interesting point that new and social media have altered the way people research and choose their employers and this is increasingly on brand, reputation, ethos and intangibles. Increasingly he is asked about CSR, volunteering, and opportunities to 'give something back'.

Graduates realise they will have to work hard, but if a firm is a slave driver, it will contribute to employees' stress and underperformance, and thus disgruntled employees and clients, and it will soon be all over the internet. Graduates select the cultural climate as well as the package and client list – they want to know what it is really like working there, and through the internet and through blogs and social media, they can find out! Obviously, one man's meat is another man's poison, but asking open questions on social media sites can help you ascertain the truth rather than just accepting the promotional company line. Social networking sites such as LinkedIn are also increasingly useful in locating opportunities and building valuable contacts.

Size of firm

The size of the organisation will make a difference to your daily work life. A smaller company may be more personal, free and entrepreneurial, and may enable you to gain broader experience and to work more closely with the senior decision-makers. However, it may also lack structure and the left hand may never know what the right hand is doing, because there are no established policies, systems and procedures. One person's bureaucracy can be another's security!

When considering working for a small company, do find out what sort of accounting software they use. If you are planning to do AAT and then enter a small practice, make sure they have the most popular accounting software, for example Quickbooks or Sage. If they are only using an Excel spreadsheet, you will not be experiencing up-to-date accounting practices, and you may also find it hard when moving company if you have no experience of these popular software packages.

If you like a lot of structure and want to know the right way of doing things, you will perhaps be better off in large organisations with clear guidelines, policies and procedures. That said, the smaller firm could afford scope for you to make your mark by putting such systems and processes in place.

Larger organisations may necessitate your taking a more specialised role, and projects may be bigger and more complex, whereas you might take a broader perspective in a smaller firm where the role may be more varied and generalist, but where the issues could perhaps be less complex and with fewer stakeholders.

Sector

Different sectors can have very different goals and focus, and therefore can give you a completely different working experience. We looked at these in detail in chapter 1, but now it's important to consider which sector may be right for you. Of course, every organisation is different, but below we have provided some generalisations about different sectors.

Obviously, commercial firms are there to maximise profits and increase market share; they are interested in the bottom line. Public, voluntary and not-for-profit organisations and NGOs are more concerned with controlling costs and effective management of funds (from taxation or donation). The pace in a non-commercial organisation may be slower, and the firm less dynamic. People may be less 'can do' and adaptable, and more 'jobsworth' in their outlook, although, this is, of course, a stereotype, and cost-cutting and the economic climate are pushing the non-commercial sector to be more efficient and professional. The public sector may suit you better should you seek a more balanced lifestyle, and it may entail more overtly worthwhile and directly socially beneficial work.

Psychologists have identified 'masculine' and 'feminine' industries and environments. This has nothing to do with sexist stereotypes and whether men or women should be working there. Some women will thrive in an aggressive, objective, 'masculine' arena (you only have to watch *The Apprentice* to witness this), and certain males are better suited to working in a nurturing, subjective, 'feminine' setting.

That said, the industries do often correspond with traditional stereotypes. 'Masculine' industries include engineering, IT, construction, telecommunications and banking, which can be quite no-nonsense and 'say it as it is', whereas 'feminine' arenas like travel, retail and hospitality may favour softer people skills and a more diplomatic approach.

This finding also has implications for the notion of a 'glass ceiling'. While it is no doubt true that sexist attitudes do to some extent prevent women reaching top roles and achieving equal pay, it has been suggested that many women choose not to continue up a 'masculine' corporate ladder, but leave to work in a smaller, more friendly business. It has further been suggested that if more women could be encouraged to join, progress and remain in 'masculine' companies, the boardroom might benefit from greater empathy, emotional intelligence and a more open climate.

Even in Public Practice, you may have to select not only the division (audit, for example) but also an industrial sector in which to specialise even before you start. You will need to be able to put forward a compelling and cohesive argument at interview as to why a certain sector – such as banking and capital markets – appeals and why you think it would suit you.

You will need to look on the firm's website at the sector divisions. PwC, for example, breaks audit sectors into:

- insurance and investment management (I&IM)

- banking and capital markets (B&CM)

- technology, information communication, entertainment and energy (TICE-Energy)

- consumer industrial products and services (CIPS).

In London, instead of the last two, the choice would be between London top tier (LTT – large companies in the FTSE 100) and London mid-tier (LMT – smaller firms). Have ready several reasons as to why you would be interested in and suited to those specialisms.

Profile: iCount

The accountancy training partnership

About us

iCount prides itself on exclusive standards of expert tuition and support for all its students. Our smaller class sizes and 24/7 one-to-one support for students set us apart from all other providers. From the first day of a course, when students are given tutors' mobile phone numbers and personal email addresses, to the day of the exam itself, when we are there at the exam centre to offer moral support to those who need it, we forge a partnership with each of our students to ensure they have the best chance of passing every exam first time. All marking of questions and course progress tests, on stages 1, 2 and 3, is done in-house by the team of highly experienced tutors, who offer detailed feedback and tips for improvement to the students every time.

The college is lavishly furnished with leather sofas, and real tea and filter coffee are available, free of charge, throughout the day in the spacious and comfortable student lounge – with skyscraper views across Manchester city centre and the distant Pennines. In the classrooms the desks are wider and deeper, the chairs are well sprung and softly padded and the latest audio-visual presentational technology means lectures make a real impact. Because we are independent and do not have the non-value-adding overheads of our larger rivals, these levels of service can be offered at prices which are up to 20% lower than theirs – delivering exclusive and market-leading levels of quality for no additional premium.

Student profile

Emma Carr is currently studying AAT level 2 at iCount Training. She was keen to improve her career prospects at work, and looked for a course that would improve her accountancy knowledge and fit in around her full-time job. iCount offers flexible learning options for the AAT – day release, afternoon or evening courses mean Emma can continue to earn while she learns and avoid any student debts from going to university.

Emma began the course in March 2011 and progressed to level 3 in September. She chose iCount as they offer the course over a shorter period – the AAT level 2 and 3 can be completed in just 12 months, and level 4 in a further 10 months. Emma was also looking for funding for her AAT, and as iCount can access government funding through our funding partner Total People, this has meant her course fees were potentially free or heavily subsidised. As the AAT is a vocational accountancy course, she is able to learn at iCount and put her knowledge into action in the workplace. Once her AAT is completed, she is keen to progress onto further studies on ACCA or CIMA.

Emma said: "Caroline is an excellent tutor and explains things well. The course is shorter than attending a mainstream college. Facilities are good, bright and clean. City-centre location – so easy to find and park!"

To find out more about iCount courses call in, ring us or visit our website.
0161 228 6564
www.icounttraining.com
16th Floor, Portland Tower, Portland Street, Manchester, M1 3LF

Qualifications and exemptions

A large consideration when deciding what route into accountancy is right for you will be whether you have the academic qualifications to get into your desired training role. Below, we'll have a look at what you may need in detail, to help you ascertain what's possible for you.

Grade requirements

Most graduate trainee accountant roles these days call for a 2.i honours degree. The selection criteria have tightened significantly over the years as more people choose to go on to university, levelling the playing field. Potential employers started to look for a higher degree classification, so everyone worked to achieve that! To differentiate, they then had to look at UCAS points, and additional relevant experience and internships, or extraordinary achievements. Relevant degrees, in, for example, finance, business and economics, are not essential but are commonly preferred.

Most employers ask for a minimum of 2.i honours and at least 280 UCAS points (87% of ACA trainees have a 2.i or first), although smaller firms and companies will consider a 2.ii. The table below shows how A levels equate to UCAS points (initially introduced as a way of quantifying grades for university entrance). An A* at A level is worth 140 points, an A 120, B 100, C 80 and so on.

There may be some flexibility. PwC, for example, run the Inspired Talent programme, which allows for lower entry grades should you be able to demonstrate excellence and 'grit' in an unrelated field, such as being an outstanding sportsperson or having led a fundraising expedition up Everest!

TABLE 5: UCAS tariffs

GCE A level and AVCE	GCE AS Double Award	GCE AS & AS VCE	POINTS VALUE
A*			140
A	AA		120
	AB		110
B	BB		100
	BC		90
C	CC		80
	CD		70
D	DD	A	60
	DE	B	50
E	EE	C	40
		D	30
		E	20

Source: www.ucas.com/students/ucas_tariff/tarifftables

A higher UCAS tariff is required for more analytical and competitive fields. As an example, PwC requirements are detailed in the graph below. The HEADstart programme, for school leavers rather than graduates, does have a marginally lower tariff requirement:

TABLE 6: PwC requirements

Service line	Qualifications required: UCAS score achieved from top three A levels or equivalent, excluding general/modern studies, and completed in one year	A level grades
Tax	300 UCAS tariff points or equivalent; 2.i degree	BBB
Assurance	300 UCAS tariff points or equivalent; 2.i degree	BBB
Financial advisory	300 UCAS tariff points or equivalent; 2.i degree	BBB
Assurance (HEADstart)	280 UCAS tariff points or equivalent	BBC
Actuarial	320 UCAS tariff points or equivalent (including Maths A level grade A); 2.i degree	ABB
Forensic technology services	300 UCAS tariff points or equivalent; 2.i degree	BBB
Strategy consulting	340 UCAS tariff points or equivalent; 2.i degree	AAB
Management consulting	340 UCAS tariff points or equivalent; 2.i degree	AAB

TABLE 6: continued …

Economic consulting	340 UCAS tariff points or equivalent (your first degree should be in economics or have a strong economics element. A second degree in economics or a related discipline can prove advantageous); 2.i degree	AAB
PwC legal	320 UCAS tariff points or equivalent; 2.i degree	ABB
Tax (HEADstart)	260 UCAS tariff points or equivalent	BCC

Source: www.pwc.com

Exemptions

The professional bodies make exemptions for relevant previous study, and some academic institutions have formally partnered with professional bodies and/ or accountancy firms. For example, Cass Business School's BSc in Accounting & Finance (City University) provides maximum exemptions and credit for prior learning from the ICAEW's Associate Chartered Accountant (ACA) qualification. The Open University (OU) Certificate in Accounting and the AAT Diploma provide exemption from all five of the CIMA Certificate levels.

It can even work the other way round. Registration with ACCA automatically provides you with registration for an Oxford Brookes BSc (Hons) in Applied Accounting. On completion of the Fundamental Skills papers F1 to F9, and the Professional Ethics module, you may submit an additional research and analysis project to Oxford Brookes University, and be assessed by the University Business School for a degree.

Exemptions are also possible between professional bodies to aid cross-qualification. For instance, you may be ACA-qualified but seek additional CIMA or CIPFA recognition. By taking two papers (Financial & Performance Reporting and Finance & Management Case Study), you could qualify in nine months for CIPFA, if already a qualified accountant (with members of the Consultative Committee of Accounting Bodies).

Exemption search

Look on the professional body websites to ascertain whether your prior courses and study provide eligibility for exemptions.

CIMA: www.cimaglobal.com/en-gb/Study-with-us/Exemptions/Exemption-search

ACCA: https://portal.accaglobal.com/accrweb/faces/page/public/accreditations/enquiry/main/EnqInstitutionsTable.jspx

CIPFA: www.cipfa.org.uk/students/prospective/exemptions.cfm

ICAEW: www.icaew.com/en/qualifications-and-programmes/aca/aca-training-in-the-uk/exams/credit-for-prior-learning/apply-for-credits-academic-qualification

Gower College Swansea
Coleg Gŵyr Abertawe

Accountancy
Part Time Courses

Designed for current or aspiring professionals

AAT is the UK's leading qualification supporting careers in accounting. It also offers a vocational, professional route to all UK Chartered and Certified accountancy qualifications (including ACCA) or degrees in accountancy.

Our professional ACCA courses are designed for current or aspiring accountancy professionals at middle and senior management in all areas of employment. We have been awarded a **Gold status** for delivery of ACCA courses.

Accountancy and Finance courses			Start date	Price
Sage Accounts	Level 1/2	AGORED	January	£200
Sage Payroll	Level 1/2	AGORED	September	£200
AAT Foundation	Level 2	AAT	September	£250
AAT Intermediate	Level 3	AAT	September or January	£300
AAT Technician	Level 4	AAT	September or January	£425
ACCA F4-F9	Level 5/6	ACCA	September	£225 per unit
ACCA P1-P2	Level 5/6	ACCA	September	£225 per unit
ACCA P3-P7	Level 6	ACCA	September	£275 per unit

Please contact Paul Sizer for more information
paul.sizer@gowercollegeswansea.ac.uk

" Because of my studies I was offered a full time position. The company want me to take over the accounts department when I qualify. **"**

Claire, AAT 4 Technician

Tycoch 01792 284000   info@gowercollegeswansea.ac.uk
www.gowercollegeswansea.ac.uk

Profile: Gower College Swansea

Gower College Swansea
Coleg Gŵyr Abertawe

Gower College Swansea was launched in August 2010, following the successful merger of Gorseinon College and Swansea College.

The merger brought together two complementary, successful organisations to create an institution that provides outstanding learning opportunities and experiences for young people, adults and employers.

Unusually for a further education institution, Gower College Swansea offers the full range of accountancy qualifications from A Level Accounts through to Association of Accounting Technicians (AAT) and Association of Chartered Certified Accountants (ACCA) courses.

We have successfully delivered AAT courses for over 20 years and ACCA for 17 years. In 2003, the college was awarded 'gold' status by the ACCA.

The accountancy teaching team at Gower College Swansea have, between them, almost 100 years of practical and management experience. All made the move into education from industry, so they know exactly what kinds of skills and qualities employers look for.

The college is very exams-focussed and has always prided itself on the high success rates achieved in the students' examinations. In 2011, under the new AAT standards, many classes achieved 100% success at the first attempt of their exams.

"Our accountancy department continues to go from strength to strength," says course co-ordinator Paul Sizer. "We cater to all kinds of students, from those who have little or no prior experience of accounts to those already working in the sector. The combination of a well-established and practically qualified teaching staff and excellent examination results makes Gower College Swansea the ideal destination for accountancy training."

Case study

Ex-Gower College Swansea student Sandra McAlister (FCCA, MABRP) qualified as a Chartered Accountant in 2002 and became a Licensed Insolvency Practitioner in 2005.

Before establishing McAlister & Co in 2007, Sandra enjoyed a successful career with a leading national insolvency firm. Working mostly in the corporate insolvency sector, Sandra has over 15 years' experience and handles all aspects of business rescue and insolvency. She is also the Chair of the ACCA network panel for Swansea and West Wales.

Sandra enrolled at Gower College Swansea in 1997 to study AAT Levels 3 and 4 before progressing onto the ACCA.

"The professional qualification which Gower College Swansea helped me obtain completely changed my employment prospects and allowed me to set up the business, which now employs 12 staff," says Sandra. "I would really encourage anyone considering an accountancy course to go for it."

"Sandra was an excellent student and has gone on to carve out a very successful career," adds course co-ordinator Paul Sizer. "In terms of things coming full circle, two of Sandra's employees are currently studying at Gower College Swansea themselves."

Ways of studying

Clearly, you can go quite a long way toward qualifying by selecting a relevant degree and gaining credits toward required practical experience and/or qualifications. However, few people will escape the hard slog of several years simultaneously studying and poring over accountancy books in the evenings, having also had a hard day at work. There will be a lot you have to learn which you know you will never use, but unfortunately, you still have to learn it.

In professional practice

The ACA qualification will usually take three years in a training contract with an authorised employer, who will customarily arrange tuition for you. If studying independently, you will need to consider a number of factors when selecting an ICAEW tuition provider:

- programme fees

- structures and combinations of courses and subjects

- how the timing of courses matches your work needs

- pros and cons of residential and non-residential courses

- level of support, assessment and feedback, and accessibility of tutors

- other resources, e.g. online learning

- vicinity of the centre and size of classes.

Traditionally, ACA training has involved a mix of weekend and weekday classroom tuition and online self-study. However, some organisations run weekend and online courses, which minimise your time out of the office. This is perhaps more important for smaller firms.

Depending on your academic entry point, Public Practice firms will support ACCA, and sometimes CIPFA and CIMA qualifications, as well.

In industry

In commerce or industry, there is equal flexibility if you are studying for CIMA, CIPFA or ACCA. Some classroom tuition is likely to be more effective for most people, and you may be supported by peers as well as tutors. Study might be during the evenings or at weekends.

First Intuition (www.firstintuition.co.uk), for example, runs classroom, online and home study courses for AAT, ACCA, CIMA, ICAEW/ACA and CPD (continuing professional development). Kaplan Financial (http://financial.kaplan.co.uk) has been a leading provider of financial training for 50 years. Similarly, BPP (www.bpp.com) is a respected provider and offers classroom tuition, virtual learning and distance learning courses leading to ACA, ACCA, CIMA and AAT.

A list of accredited training providers for each professional body may be found on the tuition provider pages of the professional bodies' websites.

With an accredited training provider, such as BUPA, Shell, Toyota, Canon or Homebase, your experience should be tailored to match the training package provided by CIMA. It is much easier to follow a training course when you are putting what you are learning into practice at work. Of course, the firms do have their own needs and agendas, so sometimes attention to the pressing company requirements may take priority. Equally, you must not allow your focus on passing examinations to prevent you from taking a broader perspective and gaining wider experience.

Costs

On formal training programmes, employers will fund your study fees and materials, and provide the required support, study leave and experience. Other employers might part fund studies, while yet others could expect you to pay for yourself, and this can be very expensive (up to £20,000), especially if already loaded down with debt from your first degree.

CIMA is currently waiving the first year's subscription for new students and some training providers may have special offers, too (for example, BPP is currently offering the first CIMA or ACCA course absolutely free to new students – conditions apply).

Accountancy scholarship

Kaplan Financial offers a scholarship worth over £15,000 to year 11 and 13 students, providing the opportunity for school leavers to study for free for their AAT and then whichever qualification they choose of ACCA, CIMA, ICAEW or CIPFA, irrespective of whether they should secure a job or funding from the government. Scholarship applications start in September, with the final selection in the spring. See http://financial.kaplan.co.uk for more information on this.

Kaplan also offers some free apprenticeship summer school placements for years 11 to 13. See http://kaplanapprenticeships.co.uk.

Business funding

AAT records show that trainees are nearly twice as likely to pass examinations if supported by their employer. A supportive firm might meet the cost of your membership, training provider fees, and study materials and books, and may even offer you a bonus or salary increase as a reward for success. Study leave and time to train have also been seen to increase pass rates. You might alert your employer to this fact and suggest the below options for how they might recoup some of their costs. Obviously, you will need to create a solid case detailing the benefits to your employer of your extending your knowledge of accounting.

Firms might apply for funding to train their staff — for example, through the Business Link, one tax practice was able to obtain 40% of the cost of putting its employees through AAT training from the Rural Development Programme, as well as getting funding for systems and software updates.

Funding for firms for AAT Foundation (NVQ level 2) and Intermediate (NVQ level 3) qualifications is also available through the apprenticeship scheme (www.apprenticeships.org.uk), which is open to all ages of trainee. Equally, foundation level funding may be obtainable from the Learning and Skills Council Train to Gain scheme (www.traintogain.gov.uk).

For funding in Scotland, Wales and Northern Ireland, see:

- www.skillsdevelopmentscotland.co.uk

- www.new.wales.gov.uk

- www.delni.gov.uk.

Obviously, the advantage of an ACA accountancy training contract is that you are earning while studying and fees are paid. For CIMA, CIPFA and ACCA, you may not be so lucky; while still working and earning, you may require some help with training costs, perhaps through a Professional and Career Development Loan (other sorts of loan are available for degree courses).

Professional and Career Development Loan

A Professional and Career Development Loan is a bank loan which does not incur interest (this is paid by the Young People's Learning Agency (YPLA) until one month after the completion of studies) or require repayment until you finish up to two years professional training, which must be deemed likely to enhance your career prospects. Interest rates may vary but currently, such loans typically have a reduced interest rate of 9.9% per annum (typical APR 5%–6%). Costs covered include 80% of course fees (100% should you have been unemployed for three months), books, travel, childcare, and even living expenses if you are working fewer than 30 hours per week.

You do need to be aged 18 or over and with at least three years residency in the UK, and intending to stay in the EU post-qualification. The course needs to lead to a standalone qualification, not one providing eligibility for the next stage, so not a foundation or access course, or the Graduate Diploma in Law (previously CPE).

Only Barclays and the Co-Op currently offer these loans – beware other banks which simply let interest accrue while you are studying.

'Time to train' requests

Should you be an employee and work for an organisation with more than 250 employees and not be employed on an official training contract, you are legally entitled to request 'time to train' when you have been employed for at least 26 weeks. Such training has to be pertinent to your professional development and role. Obviously, you should follow normal, less formal channels for requesting time and training first, and broach the subject sensitively and diplomatically with your boss.

While the employer may still pay your salary should they grant your request, they are not obliged to do so, and they might equally propose that you take unpaid study leave or work flexitime in lieu (your employer will need to consider national minimum wage and working time regulations).

To count, your 'time to train' request needs to be submitted in writing and dated. It should make clear:

- that it is a request under Section 63D of the Employment Rights Act 1996

- what the training is about

- where and when the study or training would take place

- the training provider and likely tuition and examination fees

- the qualification to which the training will lead

- how this study or training will boost your performance at work and benefit your employer's business

- whether you have made a previous request and, if so, the date of that request detailing whether it was emailed or posted.

Should you omit something, you may need to wait another year before putting in another request.

Your employer has 28 days to accept and confirm this in writing, or to arrange a meeting to thrash things out and notify you of their decision within 14 days of that (these dates can be extended by mutual consent, but this must be formally confirmed in writing). You can have a colleague or workplace union representative at the meeting (in work time and without loss of pay). Your 'witness' may confer with you but not answer on your behalf. Before the meeting you need to prepare a strong case outlining how both your performance and company's performance will be improved through such training, and how it will be provided and funded. Your employer will want to discuss how your request might practically and flexibly be accommodated, and any circumstances which might necessitate their support being withdrawn.

Should the employer agree to your request, they should formally notify you in writing, confirming what the training is about, when and where it will take place and by whom it will be supervised, the qualification, and the implications for salary and working hours, and funding responsibilities. Should you have mutually agreed to an alternative training option, this will be the one detailed and accepted. If you do not subsequently attend the agreed training you must formally notify and discuss this with your employer or they could raise a disciplinary action against you.

Your employer can reject your request (or part of the request) for one or more of the following reasons, setting out which apply and detailing key reasons why.

- Such training would not improve your performance in that company.

- It would not make their business function more effectively.

- It would create additional costs.

- It would negatively impact their ability to meet customer demand or improve quality or business performance.

- Your work cannot be delegated to existing staff.

- They are not able to recruit more staff.

- There is no work for you during proposed hours.

- The training clashes with intended structural changes.

Should your request be refused, you have 14 days to appeal — set out your case, in writing and dated. Do try talking to your manager and getting them on your side before taking any more drastic formal route. Should you be unsuccessful in your appeal, and should you feel you have been subject to discrimination, you could ultimately escalate to a tribunal, but this could obviously put paid to future progression in that company.

Profile: London School of Business & Finance

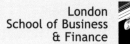

Since it was founded in 2003, the British-owned London School of Business & Finance (LSBF) has established itself as one of Europe's most innovative and dynamic business schools. With over 15,000 students from more than 150 different countries, and campuses in London, Manchester, Birmingham, Toronto and our most recently opened centre in Singapore; LSBF truly is the world's business school.

We pride ourselves on offering industry relevant programmes, with work-based learning, preparing our students to enter the world of business with advanced knowledge, practical skills and confidence. Our tutors are at the core of our success in training the business leaders of the future. We employ some of the best tutors in the industry, all with years of experience and a passion for teaching.

Our corporate network comprises over 400 multinational companies, and is integral to our continued standards of excellence. We design our programmes alongside our corporate contacts, and educational partners, ensuring that our courses always reflect wider business trends and developments.

Through our close links with big businesses, we know what blue-chip companies look for in their employees. Every student is equipped with these skills and competencies. We also give students vital work experience (with top international firms), exciting travel opportunities and access to our first-class Corporate and Careers Service. All of this gives our students a real edge in today's competitive jobs market.

At LSBF, students enjoy unparalleled flexibility; they can study full-time, part-time, online, or with a combination of on-campus and online study. Part-time courses can be taken during the day, in the evening, or at the weekend, fitting in with students' individual lifestyles and commitments. Using InterActive, our award-winning online platform, students can take complete control over their timetable, studying anytime, anywhere.

Whatever a student's career aspirations, we have a course that will help them succeed. Our portfolio of professional courses includes ACCA, CIMA, CFA® and CIM, and we also offer invaluable practical skills certificates.

We have a wide range of programmes at undergraduate and postgraduate level, focusing on finance and accountancy, management, marketing and business law, amongst other subjects.

Our new ground-breaking Trium programmes combine an undergraduate or postgraduate degree, a professional qualification and in-depth careers training. Students acquire a unique blend of knowledge and skills, giving them a real advantage over other candidates. We are so confident in the quality of our Trium programmes that we even guarantee a job offer* within six months of graduation.

Trium is just the latest example of our commitment to innovation, a commitment which is at the heart of everything we do at our business school.

At LSBF, we aim to be pioneers in business education, leading where others follow.

* See www.lsbf.org.uk for details

Case study

LSBF Student Subir Banerjee studied for an ACCA + MSc in Finance

Subir Banerjee is currently studying at the London School of Business and Finance (LSBF); taking a scholarship postgraduate degree, combined with an ACCA professional programme. Studying ACCA will give Subir invaluable practical skills, while the academic degree will equip him with the leadership and business management acumen required for a lucrative and rewarding career in business.

How did you hear about LSBF?
"I came from India to study in London at another college, but heard about the brilliant lecturers at LSBF from friends and decided to transfer. I followed them for the high standard of education that I knew I would receive at LSBF. For me, the lecturers are the most important part of a school as they add immense value to the institution."

Why did you choose to study in London?
"I've worked in India and the Middle East and realised a professional qualification would give me the push I needed to boost my career up to senior management level. I chose London for the cultural diversity, the career prospects and the number of blue-chip companies that would be nearby for me to learn from and work for when I qualify."

Tell me about your career history
"I worked in finance in the past, financial reporting as a chief accountant for a group who franchise the Western hotels. I wanted to build on this experience with some globally recognised qualifications; LSBF offered me the perfect package."

What do you hope to achieve in the future?
"The aim of doing an ACCA + MSc in Finance together is to get a deeper understanding of finance – not just number crunching. My aim is to work as a consultant in the retail sector focusing on financial reporting and studying ACCA is my route to making that happen.

"Doing an MSc adds an academic touch to my studies and once I've gained my ACCA I'll be more attractive to potential employers, especially for senior positions.

"I definitely expect to receive a higher salary once I've completed my course. Employers feel that candidates holding a combined qualification like mine are better qualified. I'd expect on average a 30-40% increase to my earning potential."

Pass rates for each professional body

While the ICAEW (ACA) examinations are said to be the most stretching, it is noteworthy that the first-time pass rate is particularly good, and their overall pass rate also one of the strongest. Of course, this may reflect the predominantly graduate intake of the highest intellectual calibre (not to mention people who are typically also particularly ambitious, competitive and driven). It could further reflect the pressure which many are under given the Public Practice 'pass or go' policy.

TABLE 7: Accountancy pass rates 2009

Qualification	First-time passes	All passes
ACCA	43%	44%
CIMA	63%	59%
CIPFA	n/a	70%
ICAEW	84%	75%
ICAI	74%	76%
ICAS	n/a	76%

Source: www.pqaccountant.com

Pass rates for 2010 repeat this pattern, with averages of ACCA 46%, CIMA 58%, CIPFA 71%, ACA 85/89%. The tables below show results (taken from the professional bodies' websites) for individual papers.

ACCA

TABLE 8: ACCA paper results December 2010

Paper	Average 48%
F1 Accountant in business	70%
F2 Management accounting	60%
F3 Financial accounting	60%
F4 Corporate and business law	44%
F5 Performance management	41%
F6 Taxation	44%

TABLE 8: continued …

F7 Financial reporting	47%
F8 Audit and assurance	38%
F9 Financial management	40%
P1 Governance, risk and ethics	51%
P2 Corporate reporting	51%
P3 Business analysis	48%
P4 Advanced financial management	33%
P5 Advanced performance management	35%
P6 Advanced taxation	44%
P7 Advanced audit and assurance	34%

Again, ACCA seems to have fared less well, and concern has been voiced because the average is down from 51% in 2008. The more complex advanced courses, which one might expect to be more difficult, mostly had pass rates of only about a third. Of course, these are advanced papers, but it may be that many of the ACCA students are not on a training contract, but studying independently with little employer support or study leave, and possibly little relevant work experience to help consolidate learning.

ACA

TABLE 9: ACA paper results December 2010 and March 2011

December 2010 paper	Average pass rate 89.2%
Accounting	83.8%
Assurance	89.5%
Principles of taxation	90.8%
Business and finance	95%
Management information	89%
Law	87.1%
March 2011 paper	**Average pass rate 85%**
Business strategy	82.2%
Financial reporting	78.9%
Financial accounting	87.5%
Audit and assurance	80.2%
Taxation	91.7%
Financial management	81.3%
Financial accounting top up	93.8%

ACA consistently achieves the highest pass rates out of all of the accounting qualifications, which does not reflect an easier syllabus. Besides being candidates of the highest calibre, they are also very well trained, crammed and supported.

What happens if you fail?

In 2009, a ranting email from a PwC trainee, who had been asked to leave because he failed his ACA examinations, went viral. A PwC spokesperson simply commented: 'At the end of the three years, we look at their performance over the three years very carefully and if they have not met the required standard, they would be asked to leave.' The significant factor may be your 'performance over the three years'.

KPMG makes a similar comment on its website: 'KPMG values its people. We give our trainees the best support available prior to the exams and so our exam failure rate is low. However, in the event that trainees do fail they are given the opportunity of a resit subject to meeting certain criteria.' 'Subject to meeting certain criteria' may perhaps be akin to 'performance over the three years', but it may also take into account how badly you have failed.

The training contract will no doubt state that the firm has the right to terminate employment due to examination failure, and some firms will indeed enforce this, but others may allow you one chance at a resit. You are likely to have to fund this yourself and you may not be afforded study leave. Of course, it is best to check all this out during the application stage.

Should you fail and be required to leave, then that could be a good time to see a career consultant to devise a 'plan B'. Should you consider a different field of accountancy, or a different firm, sector or professional body? Was accountancy ever the right thing? Could you have been more motivated in a different specialism? Could you have studied harder? Did personal circumstances interfere and contribute to poor performance? Some firms may even be prepared to fund career counselling as a goodwill gesture on your leaving.

CIPFA

The average pass rate for CIPFA is 71%, which is particularly laudable considering that the intake is not so selective – you only need two A levels to study for CIPFA qualifications. The lowest pass rate (just 56%) was for the governance and public policy paper, but exam failure is unlikely to lead to you losing your job in the public sector.

TABLE 10: CIPFA paper results June 2009 and December 2010

December 2010 paper	Average pass rate 71%
Financial reporting	71%
Management accounting	73%
Financial, management systems and techniques	66%
Financial accounting	82%
Audit and assurance	85%
Leadership and management	69%
Financial and performance reporting	63%
Governance and public policy	56%
Accounting for decision making	70%
Public finance	75%
Taxation	76%
Finance and management case study	64%
Strategic business management	78%
Final test June 2009	**Cycle 2**
Number of portfolios	78%
Submits	67%
Pending/reworks	11%
Audit and assurance	80.2%
Submit %	86%

CIMA

CIMA students scored slightly higher than ACCA trainees, averaging a 58% pass rate, perhaps in similar circumstances. Interestingly, the pass rate was highest for financial operations – the field, perhaps, where accountants would have more day-to-day, hands-on experience.

TABLE 11: CIMA paper results December 2010

Operational and management levels	Average pass rate 58%
P1 – performance operations	46%
P2 – performance management	52%
E1 – enterprise operations	63%
E2 – enterprise management	46%
F1 – financial operations	72%
F2 – financial management	56%
Strategic level	
P3 – performance strategy	60%
E3 – enterprise strategy	61%
F3 – financial strategy	57%
T4 part B case study examination (includes March and May 2010 PC exams)	68%

Learning at Your Fingertips

Decide where, when and how you learn

ICS offer a flexible way to study for your CIMA qualification - the world's largest professional body of management accountants.

We offer the entry level accounting qualification 'Certificate in Business Accounting' for students with little or no accounting background – it's a recognised qualification which is valued by employers.

Papers 1- 5

- Fundamentals of:
  - Management Accounting
  - Financial Accounting
  - Business Mathematics
  - Business Economics
  - Ethics, Corporate Governance and Business Law

As experts in distance learning we will support you every step of the way and you'll receive CIMA approved study materials, including the CIMA Official Learning System, the only test written and endorsed by CIMA. To find out more visit **icslearn.co.uk** or call **0800 015 8064** to speak to an experienced course advisor.

find out more

0800 015 8064
icslearn.co.uk

Profile: ICS Learning

Start your career in Accountancy with Distance Learning

If there was ever any doubt that money makes the world go round, the events of the previous few years have proved it to be true. The role of financial experts is more important than ever, and for anyone with ambitions to pursue a career in accountancy, a proper grounding in how financial systems drive business is crucial.

A recognised qualification will do more than just get your foot in the door. Joanne McManus, Operations Director at ICS, the world's most experienced distance learning organisation, stresses that proper guidance and tutoring can help prepare people for the world of work beyond academic requirements.

ICS currently supports students through the five-part Chartered Institute of Management Accountants (CIMA) Certificate in Business Accounting, the entry-level course for those pursuing an accounting role. The course not only provides the fundamental skills needed for a career in finance, but also the opportunity to work around existing learning, work or home commitments.

Joanne McManus explains that "distance learning puts the knowledge at students' fingertips and allows them to manage their studies at their own pace at any time of day. This can be hugely important for people who are already working, have families to support or other commitments which make it more difficult to attend classes at set times, or a set location.

"Our students also have access to expert tutors who can talk them through the requirements of the course and help them relate that to real-world experience. Then, when the students are ready to enter their first job they are better-equipped for how their academic learning relates to the world of work."

The CIMA course covers:

- fundamentals of management accounting

- fundamentals of financial accounting

- fundamentals of business mathematics

- fundamentals of business economics

- fundamentals of ethics, corporate governance and business law.

As part of the course, students will receive CIMA-approved study materials including the CIMA Official Learning System, and tests that will fully prepare you for the CIMA exams.

Julie Hepburn, Education Services Director says "distance learning should be flexible and fit around a student's lifestyle; everyone has a range of priorities to attend to. We're keen that learning doesn't become a burden but rather a rewarding way to improve career prospects. Accountancy is a challenging, rewarding career and learning the fundamentals is a very important part of building the skills needed to progress in the profession."

For more information visit **icslearn.co.uk** or call 0800 015 8064 to speak to an experienced course adviser.

Case study

Economist Janet Hontoir says there's nothing more conducive to successful study than proper support – which is why she's spent 12 years of her working life helping ICS students embark on their own careers in accountancy.

Janet, who is 61, has been a tutor with distance learning specialists ICS since 1999. A key part of her role is to support students through their studies on the ICS CIMA Certificate in Business Accounting course, which is an entry level programme for those pursuing an accounting career. Her role brings her into contact with students from all walks of life, but they all share the same desire for the flexibility offered by distance learning.

As a highly experienced economist, South Wales-based Janet has taught at a number of further and higher education colleges and universities. However, she says that the accessibility of distance learning is making it more and more attractive to busy individuals.

Janet says "the beauty of distance learning is that it offers a flexible approach to education and allows students to learn at their own pace. Students can commit to as many or as few course modules as they want and studying can also be worked in around other personal and work commitments – that is an attractive proposition for everyone."

Janet has been involved in teaching for nearly 40 years, but says the feeling of accomplishment she receives from helping a student pass an exam or solve a problem is as strong today as it was at the beginning of her career.

"We have a vast range of students from different backgrounds studying with us including young professionals, academics and business owners. Some students even study with us in order to help reintroduce themselves to the education system, increase personal expertise or simply to boost their confidence.

"I have regular discussions with my students over email or telephone and offer guidance about all aspects of the course, whether it is coursework advice and feedback, study techniques or general course queries – it is a successful combination and produces good results."

Julie Hepburn, Education Services Director at ICS explains that "accountancy is a popular career choice but it's a very competitive market so quality education is important. ICS aims to meet all of its students' needs by providing the complete package. This includes good quality course materials, easy accessibility and excellent tutor support."

For more information on ICS's CIMA courses please visit: **www.icslearn.co.uk/ qualifications/cima**

Study tips

Of course, all examinations are difficult if you have not put in sufficient effort, but they can be easy and relatively stress-free when you have really learned the material. Some people are plodders, who have to work very hard to achieve the same results as others, who always seem to just 'wing it' and do well. Certain people work almost too hard, because they are perfectionists or so afraid of failure that they cannot find the right balance, and this can be self-defeating. However, almost everyone who trains in accountancy, even the brightest graduate, would say that working full pelt while studying for professional qualifications is darned hard and you must be totally disciplined.

Set yourself a timetable

Make sure that you manage your time effectively and prioritise. Which examinations are you due to take first? Get organised with a study plan and a timetable for coursework, revision and practice papers. Remember to add some breaks, leisure time and rewards for hard work into the picture – create balance.

Create a routine

The timetable should help you stick to a study routine. When are the days you will be with the tuition providers? Are you a morning or evening person? Would you be better getting up a few hours earlier and studying before work, rather than in the evening when tired? Do not just spend all day on a Sunday working – short bursts tend to be more productive. Make a certain time your study period and let family and friends know that you will not be available to come out to play, or even be contactable at those times – turn off the mobile.

Create a study space

It can be difficult when sharing a flat with several other young professionals, but try to create a quiet and comfortable space where you can study undisturbed. Do you really work best with that music at full blast? Keep the door shut to prevent people wandering in for a chat.

How do you learn best?

Are you linear or 'big picture' in your thinking? Linear people like lists and do things serially, whereas holistic people may learn better using mind maps.

Find a study partner

Some people prefer to study alone, but you could link up with a fellow trainee from your course or workplace and work on topics together. Talking to and teaching each other should help you consolidate learning, as well as providing mutual support when it all feels too much.

Don't be too proud to ask for help

Top graduates are often unaccustomed to struggling. You may feel that you are failing or disappointing people, or not living up to previous academic successes. If you do not immediately grasp something, be prepared to ask questions and to speak with the tutor, or perhaps have a work colleague explain something. You will look more foolish if you fail. That said, accountancy examinations are notoriously hard and very few trainees sail through passing everything first time.

Make the most of tutors, study and revision materials

Tuition providers have a reputation to uphold; they want you to pass and they should have created some valuable materials. They should also make themselves available to help and may even link with your employer should extra time or assistance be necessary. Tuition providers usually offer revision programmes and practice examinations. CIPFA has its own exam skills course. Make the most of any study leave – don't waste the time and then cram madly at the last minute.

Practice papers

You cannot always predict what will come up, but practice papers will enable you to familiarise yourself with the type of questions and identify knowledge gaps. They are, of course, good for going over things and revising what you know. If they seem easy, you should gain in confidence.

Examination day

Have a good night's sleep and a hearty breakfast. Arrive early with everything you need. Relax. Read the question carefully – several times. Manage your time – how long do you have for each question? Which questions will take longer? If you run out of time for a question, try to at least jot down the salient points – if you do not have time to go back to it, you may at least have earned some marks. Which can you do easily and get out of the way? Which earn the most marks? Remember, if you have studied hard and learnt the work, you have nothing to fear! If those other 300,000 qualified accountants could do it, so can you!

4

The Training Contract

What is a Training Contract?

A Training Contract is distinct from an employment contract. It is a signed agreement between the trainee and employer. The Training Contract outlines the terms and conditions of the training to be provided and in turn details the criteria which you will also need to meet to remain eligible. Such contracts are commonly used when the employer is to fund external training by a third party provider. To study for ACA, you must have a Training Contract; you may also find that firms providing external and internal training for CIMA, AAT or ACCA trainees offer Training Contracts too.

For all ACA or ACCA qualifications with the Big Four and most other Public Practice firms, Training Contracts are mandatory.

Depending on your entry point, the Training Contract will last one to five years, but three years is typical for the average graduate. Training will include hands-on work experience, internal training and external tuition for examinations. You will be working and earning, as well.

The typical terms and conditions of a three-year Training Contract are:

- the firm will provide training, to include all tuition, examination and institute subscription fees

- the trainee employee must study in their own time (although block study periods are often part of the training)

- the trainee employee's training and employment contracts will be terminated should they fail an exam more than once, or fail seriously (usually 45% or below, where the pass mark for the paper is 55%).

Work experience and study components

Accountancy training combines practical work experience with theoretical study, and an accredited training employer will contract to provide you with both. Obviously, studies seem more relevant and are more readily consolidated when you actually apply what you are learning in work, and you will need to demonstrate your capability on the job, too. However, for ACCA and CIMA, the practical performance monitoring and experience component do not need to be completed simultaneously.

Differing syllabuses and practical requirements

Before entering into a Training Contract, it's important to be very clear about what the contract includes, and what it doesn't. Below, we will examine in detail what your potential employer is actually paying for and its value. We also show how the employer should ensure that your practical experience is in sync with the study modules. You'll see that the different professional bodies have different requirements, to match their slightly different emphasis or slant.

We've also listed the costs of the qualifications. These will normally be paid by your employer, but you may have to pay for resits, so it's good to have an idea of the costs involved. Your contract should specify what your employer will and will not pay and you should understand this fully, and any financial implications this could have.

ACA (ICAEW)

Syllabus

The syllabus consists of two parts:

1. the Professional Stage (technical knowledge modules and core competencies underpinning accountancy, combined with a more applied, practical element)

2. the Advanced Stage (two more complex technical papers and a case study). There is clearly quite a technical emphasis, befitting the initial Public Practice bias. The table below shows the structure in greater detail.

Table 12: ACA syllabus structure – Advance Stage

Two technical integration papers and one case study		
Ethics	Case study (C)	
Ethics	Technical integration	Business change (BC)
Ethics	Technical integration	Business reporting (BR)

Table 13: ACA syllabus structure – Advanced Stage

12 papers (six knowledge and six application)			
Application level		*Knowledge level*	
Ethics	Audit and assurance (AA)	Ethics	Assurance (AS)
Ethics	Business strategy (BS)	Ethics	Business and finance (BF)
Ethics	Financial reporting (FR)	Ethics	Law
Ethics	Taxation (TX)	Ethics	Principles of taxation
Financial accounting (FA)		Accounting (AC)	
Financial management (FM)		Management information (M1)	

Practical componet

For ACA qualification, there is a requirement of 450 7-hour days of technical work experience, which you must document in hard copy on the appropriate form (ETWE). This involves your undertaking hands-on commercial or financial experience in audit and assurance, tax, management accounting or financial reporting and so on, with six-monthly reviews. With prior work experience and qualification, you may be able to claim up to one year's credits, reducing the work experience requirement to 300 days. All your experience may be in one of six categories or specialism (audit experience is not obligatory and needs to be recorded separately), but sufficient depth, breadth and progression will need to be demonstrated, perhaps through secondments.

TABLE 14: Examples of common areas of practical activity and technical work experience

Accounting	Audit/assurance	Taxation
Financial accounting	Company audit	Corporate tax compliance
Management accounting	Assurance assignments	Personal tax compliance
• Recording financial transactions and investigating and correcting errors in books of account	Other external audit	PAYE, NIC, VAT
	Internal audit	Tax planning and advice
	• Planning, controlling and recording audit/assurance work	Personal financial planning
• Preparing management reports		• Analysis of income, expenditure and other relevant data
• Preparing financial statements including consolidations	• Assessing adequacy of accounting systems	• Preparation of personal and corporate tax returns and computations
• Applying relevant Financial Reporting Standards, Companies Acts, Stock Exchange and other requirements to financial statements	• Gathering and evaluating audit evidence	
	• Evaluating and testing internal controls	• Preparation of returns and administration of PAYE/NIC, VAT and other excise duties
• Preparing and reviewing budgets, comparison against performance, profit and cashflow forecasts	• Reviewing financial statements	
	• Applying auditing standards and guidelines	• Communications with tax authorities
• Designing and installing management accounting information and control systems	• Compliance with regulatory body requirements	• Other work to ensure compliance with statutory tax obligations
• Forensic accounting	• Drafting audit and similar reports	• Tax planning reviews
• Preparing accountant's reports for small companies (in lieu of audit reports)	• Use of IT in any of the above	• Back duty/in-depth investigations
		• Dealing with investments, pensions and trusts
• Use of IT in any of the above		• Carrying out fiscal valuations
		• Use of IT in any of the above
Financial management	**Insolvency**	**Information technology**
Treasury	Administration	Systems analysis
Investment and financing decisions	Receivership	Systems design and programming
Business process change	Liquidation	Systems selection and implementation
Resource management	• Preparing statements of affairs	IT support
Company secretarial	• Realisation of assets	• Carrying out general controls and application reviews
Corporate finance	• Proving debtors and creditors	
Corporate advisory services	• Completing statutory returns	

Financial management	Insolvency	Information technology
• Evaluating investment proposals • Choosing and obtaining sources of finance • Management of borrowings, cash and other liquid resources • Debtor and creditor management • Formulating corporate structures and business plans • Changing business processes and information systems • Analysing and interpreting financial information • Preparing investigation reports/ circulars • Foreign exchange transactions • Non-fiscal valuations • Investigation and due diligence • Use of IT in any of the above	• Meetings procedures • Use of IT in any of the above	• Changing business processes and information systems • Interrogations using computer-aided audit techniques • Evaluating hardware and software • Security reviews • Disaster and contingency planning • Design of databases, networks and communications links • Training of users and operators

Source: www.icaew.com

Examinations

Unless you are an independent student, a training organisation will typically pay exam entry fees (and tuition fees) on your behalf. There are two types of examinations.

E-assessments, completed on a computer
You are not restricted to specific exam dates, which affords you and your employer greater flexibility in matching study and assessment timetables with work schedules and business needs. ICAEW-accredited test centres may be tutorial organisations or the Pearson Vue dedicated test centres (www.pearsonvue.co.uk).

- Exams are taken at your chosen ICAEW-accredited training centre.

- Exams last 1½ hours and require a pass mark of 55%.

- If necessary, you may resit the exam immediately (perhaps following discussion with your employer).

- You should receive results the following day.

Paper-based examinations, i.e. Professional Stage application modules and
Advanced Stage examinations

- Exams are set and marked by the ICAEW.

- Professional Stage exams last 2½ hours, have a pass mark of 55%, and are taken in March, June, September and December.

- Advanced Stage Technical Papers last 3½ hours with a pass mark of 50%, and are taken in July and November.

- Advanced Stage Case Study exams last 4 hours, have a pass mark of 50%, and are taken in July and November.

- ICAEW allows four attempts for each Professional Stage module, but your employer may have their own (lesser) limit. The ICAEW has removed the limit for the number of tries at Advanced Stage.

Costs and fees

Tuition fees will vary by provider (there can be substantial differences, even £300 to £800 on certain modules) and fees may not be readily advertised on websites, because these are usually paid by the employer and no doubt negotiable. Fees for resits may be listed, because you may have to fund yourself if retaking.

A London-based tuition provider (lists of tuition providers may be found on the ICAEW site) might charge about £300 for each of the six knowledge modules, £600 for the six application modules and £700 for the three Advanced Stage components. The total amount might be at least £7,335. These prices exclude VAT (the total would be £8,802 including VAT at 20%), and do not include ICAEW study materials.

Professional Stage study materials cost £30 per knowledge module, and £45 per application module. Advanced Stage Technical Integration modules incur a cost of £140 for the double study pack, and the case study is £70. Thus, you need to add another £660.

On top of this, there would be ICAEW/ACA examination and student fees. Student fees are £165 (plus VAT) per annum. Each knowledge module costs £65 and each application module £85 (exemptions cost the same). The Technical Integration modules each cost £165 and the case study £255. Additional fees are therefore £1,950 before VAT.

The total before VAT is £9,945 over the three years, assuming no failures and resits (each costing approximately £260 plus VAT), and not including any revision courses (for each module about £340 plus VAT), or practice examinations. Fees will no doubt also be subject to an annual increase.

ACCA

Syllabus

The syllabus comprises theoretical and practical assessment. It covers both Public Practice and business issues.

- Fourteen examinations need to be passed within 10 years (see table below).

- Thirteen performance objectives need to be monitored and met by an appointed workplace mentor, but this could be before, after or during studies. There is no time limit for gaining the required three years of practical work experience.

TABLE 15: ACCA SYLLABUS STRUCTURE

Fundamentals level		Professional level	
Knowledge module	*Skills module*	*Essential module*	*Options module – two of four papers (3-hour paper-based D exams)*
F1 Accountant in business	F4 Corporate and business law	P1 Governance risk and ethics	P4 Advanced financial management
F2 Management accounting	F5 Performance management	P2 Corporate reporting	P5 Advanced performance management
F3 Financial accounting	F6 Taxation	P3 Business analysis	P6 Advanced taxation
	F7 Financial reporting		P7 Advanced audit and assurance
	F8 Audit and assurance		
	F9 Financial management		

Practical component

For the ACCA practical component you will be required to achieve 13 performance objectives in total:

- all nine 'essentials' – performance objectives 1 to 9
- any four 'options' – performance objectives 10 to 20.

ACCA lists these as follows.

Professionalism, ethics and governance

1. Ethics, values and judgement in application

2. Contribute to the effective governance of an organisation

3. Raise awareness of non-financial risk

Personal effectiveness

4. Manage self

5. Effective communication

6. Use of ICT

Business management

7. Manage ongoing activities in your area of responsibility

8. Improvement of departmental performance

9. Management of an assignment

Financial accounting and reporting

10. Prepare financial statements for external purposes

11. Interpret financial transactions/statements

Performance measurement and management accounting

12. Preparation of financial information for management

13. Contribution to budget planning and production

14. Monitor and control budgets

Finance and financial management

15. Evaluate potential business/investment opportunities and the required finance options

16. Manage cash using active cash management and treasury systems

Audit and assurance

17. Prepare for and collect evidence for audit

18. Evaluate and report on audit

Taxation

19. Evaluate and compute taxes payable

20. Assist with tax planning

Examinations

Depending on your educational and vocational experience, you may be exempt from initial papers, but most trainees are required to pass a total of 14 exams. These are a mixture of computer-based exams (CBEs – taken any time to suit) and paper-based exams (PBEs – taken in June and December). There are 400 ACCA exam centres around the world.

You may resit as many times as you like (assuming that your employer is agreeable and within the 10-year limit).

Costs and fees

Besides the ACCA membership subscription and examination fees, there are substantial training costs. London-based training providers can charge £400 to £700 for each course module including materials and tuition, plus an additional £500 to £600 for the revision courses, and a further £245 for the examination rehearsal. So, given that there are 16 modules, qualifying is not cheap and the value of a Training Contract quickly becomes evident. Over the three years, the fees with one such provider could total £19,690. Fees will no doubt also be subject to increases annually and perhaps additional VAT. You do need to shop around though, because these fees can vary substantially, and some tuition providers may include a free practice exam with a revision course.

In addition to this, ACCA charges fees of £72 for registration and three years subscriptions at £72 a year. The three knowledge examinations cost £57 each, the six skills examinations £72 each, the seven professional components £84 each. This gives a total of £1,479.

Thus, the cost of qualifying (assuming first-time passes) could be more than £21,000 spread over the three years. However, revision courses and practice exams are clearly optional.

CIMA

Syllabus

Table 14 shows the syllabus and modules for CIMA qualification. To achieve chartered status (ACMA – Associate Chartered Management Accountant) you must pass all levels. The initial Certificate Level includes five modules, and the subsequent Professional Level involves three modules, each with operational, managerial and strategic level components (nine in total). The final stage, T4, includes research, application of knowledge and report-writing for a fictional case study. There are no time restrictions.

TABLE 16: CIMA SYLLABUS STRUCTURE

T4 (formerly TOPCIMA) Test of Professional Competence in Management Accounting	CIMA Professional Qualification (ACMA status)			Certificate in Business Accounting (CBA)
Students must be able to:	*Operational level*	*Management level*	*Strategic level*	*Exemptions from this stage are possible with an accounting degree or AAT qualification*
• carry out focused research of a news industry in detail	E1 Enterprise operations	E2 Enterprise management	E3 Enterprise strategy	C01 Fundamentals of management accounting
• relate fictional companies' issues to technical knowledge	P1 Performance operations	P2 Performance management	P3 Performance strategy	C02 Fundamentals of financial accounting
• produce professional reports under examination conditions, incorporating and applying the research	F1 Financial operations	F2 Financial management	F3 Financial strategy	C03 Fundamentals of business mathematics
				C04 Fundamentals of business economics
				C05 Fundamentals of ethics, corporate governance and business law

Practical component

Additionally, you will need at least three years' relevant work-based practical experience before qualifying as a chartered management accountant. Some or all this experience may be obtained before embarking on CIMA studies (where internships and vacation work, for example, can be valuable). On a formal training scheme, the employer should ensure that you receive the correct balance of experience. The CIMA website lists required practical experience as follows; it may be drawn and recorded from any of the three sections, but must include at least 18 months of core activities.

CIMA lists Core Practical Experience Activities as follows.

Area 1: basic experience

1a. Preparing and maintaining accounting records

1b. Statutory and regulatory reporting

1c. IT desktop skills

1d. Systems and procedure development

Area 2: core experience

2a. Preparation of management accounts

2b. Planning, budgeting and forecasting

2c. Management reporting for decision-making

2d. Product and service costing

2e. Information management

2f. Project appraisal

2g. Project management

2h.   Working capital content

2i.   Risk management and business assurance

Area 3: supplementary experience

3a.   Financial strategy

3b.   Corporate finance

3c.   Treasury management

3d.   Taxation

3e.   Business evaluation and appraisal

3f.   Business strategy

3g.   External relationships

Examinations

A series of rules govern when and where examinations are taken, as follows.

- CIMA Certificate in Business Accounting examinations may be taken any time at an approved training centre.

- All CIMA Professional Module (operational, management and strategic level) examinations must be taken at CIMA-approved locations at set times of the year (May and November, with resit exams in March and September).

- The T4 – Test of Professional Competence in Management Accounting (Topcima) paper-based or computer-based examination component (as opposed to the practical element) may be taken in March, May, September and November.

Costs and fees

Again, if self-funding, you will be in for a substantial cost, because there are 15 modules in total which, with a London-based tuition provider, may cost as much as

£500 to £670 each (£1,440 for T4), plus £500 to £600 for the revision programmes and £245 for the practice examination. Over three years, the cost of these modules could be as much as £17,615, although revision courses and practice exams could be omitted. This does not take into account any annual fee increases or additional VAT.

There are also CIMA fees to consider. The first year's subscription is free, but you will still be in for registration, subsequent subscriptions (which go up to £210 on completion of T4 part B), and examination fees (exemption fees, should these be appropriate, are the same price as for the examination modules). Thus, you would additionally need to pay £63 to register, two years' subscription at £94, five certificate modules at £45 each, six operational and management modules at £75 each, three strategic level examinations at £81 each, and £101 for the T4. This comes to another £1,270.

Assuming that you are able to pass everything first time, you will still need to find approximately £18,885 over the three years.

CIPFA

Syllabus

Qualifications again take three years and are divided into three parts: certificate, diploma and final test of professional competence. They have been designed in consultation with employers to dovetail with trainees' work placements and with the hands-on skills which they acquire.

- The certificate (CIPFA affiliate membership) includes examination in financial accounting, management accounting, financial reporting, and financial management systems and techniques.

- The diploma (CIPFA associate membership) covers audit and assurance, leadership and management, decision-making accounting, governance and public policy, financial and performance reporting, public finance, and taxation.

- The final test of professional competence (full CIPFA membership) examines strategic business management and a case study in finance and management.

TABLE 17: CIPFA syllabus structure

The CIPFA Certificate (affiliate membership)	The CIPFA Diploma (associate membership)		Final Test of Professional Competence (full CIPFA membership)
Financial accounting (FA)	Accounting and decision-making (ADM)	Audit and assurance (A&A)	Strategic business management (SBM)
Financial management systems and techniques (FMST)	Leadership and management (L&M)	Financial and performance reporting (F&PR)	Financial and management case study
Financial reporting (FR)	Public finance (PF)	Governance and public policy (G&PP)	
Management accounting (MA)	Taxation (T)		

Practical component

CIPFA provides comprehensive guidance notes on the practical component of training, the Initial Professional Development Scheme (IPDS). You can read or download these in full at www.cipfa.org.uk/students/current/download/IPDS_guide_aug06.pdf.

You are required to produce a four-part portfolio demonstrating professional development.

1. A log of validated work experience (400 days).

2. Recorded evidence of application and reflection on three of the following:

    -   leadership and strategic management
    -   strategic and operational financial management
    -   financial and performance reporting
    -   governance, ethics and values
    -   audit and accountability
    -   partnerships and stakeholder relations
    -   change, risk and project management
    -   procurement and contract management.

3. For the final test of professional competence:

   - planning, preparation, delivery and reflection on an oral presentation
   - ability to manage an iterative process
   - management of a long-term planned process.

4. Reflective commentary on work experience and professional development and goals.

Through an hour-long interview, an assessor will aim to confirm that work documented is accurate, true, and, indeed, your own. You should receive your results within three weeks.

Examinations

The two sittings of all examinations take place in June and November or December at set venues. Certificate and diploma stage exams are all three hours long, other than two half papers at the diploma stage (on public finance and taxation), which last two hours.

Costs and fees

Again, costs will vary greatly according to the training provider and the method of learning (personal tuition, group classes or online). London-based training providers often quote about £1,000 per course and there are 13 modules. However, with CIPFA itself, you are looking at roughly £600 for each module (and £1,500 for the final case study), plus £225 per revision course and £50 for the exam essentials, totalling perhaps £11,370 over the three years. Revision courses and practice exams could be omitted, of course.

CIPFA fees need to be counted, too. Initial registration is £50 and annual student subscription £151 per year (half price if joining after 1 July). Exemptions are £100 per module and examination fees for the certificate or diploma stage £90 per module. The final tests of competence and portfolio submissions are £200 each. Thus, you are looking at another £50, three yearly subscriptions at £151, 11 modules at £90 and three further payments of £200, which comes to £2,093 without any retakes or resubmissions.

In all, you are looking at a cost of £13,463 over the three years. Fees will also be subject to increases over the three years and perhaps added VAT.

Additional in-house training offered

Besides such professional skills and knowledge courses run by external training providers, you are likely to be put through induction programmes and internal courses. UHY Hacker Young group, for instance, runs courses in accounting, auditing and business-speak in the first two weeks after you join. Similarly, Blick Rothenberg provides early basic grounding in accounting and audit, and besides such technical training, the group offers you personal and management development courses to build skills such as assertiveness, negotiating and team-working.

Deloitte, which claims to have a strong learning and development team, also runs intensive internal courses; again, these deal with initial technical training in audit, and business skills topics like personal impact, coaching and client relationships. Some courses are e-learning programmes (over 4,000 e-learning units via the Skillsoft platform), while others involve simulations, residential facilitator-led training and workshops, but primarily classroom-based to ensure that you have the support on hand when you require it.

Besides such induction courses, firms are likely to offer a variety of CPD options to meet your longer-term professional development requirements.

5

Alternative routes into accountancy

On-the-job training

Not everyone wants or is able to attend university, and the raising of university fees will certainly mean that students are increasingly looking for alternative routes into a career. If you have strong A level grades (280 UCAS points) and have already decided that accountancy is the right career for you, if you are considering a career change, or if you have failed to meet the graduate recruitment criteria, there are on-the-job training schemes. These can speed up the process of professional qualification, so you could be ACCA-qualified within just four years.

PwC runs the HEADstart programme. In the assurance stream, you would be working on clients' sites on real audit projects and managing your own workload immediately, checking financial records, collating company information, attending stock counts, and testing controls. You would be supported and mentored through training, studying and working simultaneously and would have the same opportunities as graduate entrants once qualified. The option of further study toward the Oxford Brookes degree (mentioned on p135) also remains.

There is also a tax stream alternative. Requiring 260 UCAS points, this leads to an Association of Tax Technicians (ATT) qualification after two years, and CTA exams in your fourth year to become a chartered tax adviser.

KPMG has just introduced a similar six-year programme which enables you to train while in salaried employment, progressing to professional qualifications and a degree. Grade requirements are ABB grades at A level, plus B grades in GCSE maths and English language (or equivalent).

Similarly, Deloitte offers the BrightStart School Leaver programme, where you would be thrown in at the deep end and working in client-facing roles from day one, while studying for examinations and attending internal training events. Your work would vary according to the business area, which might be audit (analysing, interpreting and testing data and processes), information and technology risk (identifying risk, looking for unusual trends and 'ethical hacking', testing and making control recommendations), tax (completing returns, working with Customs & Excise, advising on pricing, and finding tax solutions), or reorganisation services (analysing data, market research, generating insolvency solutions, preparing reports and presentations).

Obviously, there are pros and cons for school leaver entry. On the plus side, you will not incur student debts and you can gain valuable experience while studying. You could always go on to further or higher education at a later stage. On the negative side, you may feel that you are committing to a profession very early and you would miss out on the social and personal development aspects of university life. You would also lack the graduate status, credibility and marketability which has become so important over recent years (although this may change should fewer people go on to tertiary education due to the fee increase).

Editorial: Golding Computer Services

Learn whilst you earn – on-the-job training – QCF accredited qualifications

golding computer services

With a background of 29 years' experience as a Sage on-the-job training provider, Golding Computer Services, working closely with Sage and the International AB, has developed a range of **On-the-Job** Computerised Accounting for Business Distance Learning Courses which can be undertaken either at home or in the workplace.

Over 300,000 employers in the UK rely on Sage Computerised Accounting programs to look after their bookkeeping needs and to run their organisations efficiently. Research has disclosed that 63% of employees who use computerised accounts programs have no formal qualifications.

Having listened to Employers' concerns, Sage, the UK's leading Accounting Software provider, and the International Association of Bookkeepers have collaborated to develop a new range of QCF Accredited Qualifications – **Computerised Accounting for Business**, Levels 1, 2 and 3.

With no educational attainment specified to study for the qualifications, the new courses present an excellent opportunity, at any age, to undertake training in the skills employers require and attain a recognised QCF accredited qualification.

There are excellent career opportunities available as bookkeepers and accountants in business. Frequently, organisations are looking for future managers when they recruit accountancy trainees, and expect them one day to manage their own departments and supervise the work of other staff.

Many top managers and directors have a financial background and a thorough understanding of business finance provides an ideal platform for entrepreneurs or anyone wishing to start their own business.

Golding Computer Services is an accredited IAB Training Centre which has worked in partnership with Sage and the IAB, to develop, on-line supported, distance learning courses for Levels 1, 2 and 3 of the IAB Computerised Accounting for Business QCF qualifications.

The IAB and Sage have teamed up to provide a compelling combination in a single 'package' available now, for studying at home or in the workplace, through Golding Computer Services. The courses include:

- registration for an innovative IAB qualification, accredited to the QCF by Ofqual, in Computerised Accounting for Business (at Levels 1,2 or 3)
- student Membership of the IAB
- Sage Learning Materials, published by Sage and approved by the IAB as being tailored to meet the content and assessment requirements for these qualifications
- a copy of Sage 50 Accounts Professional, free to use for 180 days
- an additional certificate issued by Sage, to further endorse the competence demonstrated by those who achieve the IAB qualification
- a specially trained tutor who can offer support on-line, by phone or by email.

If you wish to find out more about these courses and other **On-the-Job** IAB and Sage Bookkeeping and Payroll courses or Book-keeping Apprenticeships, please contact training@goldings.info

Accounting technicians

You would not require any formal qualifications for a position as a trainee accounting technician, but employers will be looking for evidence of:

- good written and oral communication skills

- ability to work in a team, alongside accounting professionals

- ability to multi-task and manage your time

- strong numeracy

- good attention to detail

- IT literacy.

Previous relevant study and work experience will obviously add weight to a CV when you are applying for traineeships. Qualification as an accounting technician is an excellent basic foundation and provides credits from professional accountancy qualifications. The main qualifications are as follows.

Association of Accounting Technicians (AAT) qualification

AAT (www.aat.org.uk) is a professional membership body sponsored by the other professional chartered accountancy bodies, CIMA, CIPFA, ICAS and ICAEW. It has a global membership of 120,000.

The AAT accounting qualification has value in its own right, but is often used as a stepping stone or foundation for professional accountancy qualifications. All the above professional bodies offer exemptions on the first stages of their professional examinations. As an accounting technician, you would usually start in a support role, and you could work in all the same sectors as accountants (Public Practice, commerce, industry and public sector). You might work in accounts, bookkeeping, credit control, payroll and audit, controlling budgets and resources, and you might even become self-employed and provide accounts and taxation advice to SMEs. Many companies, including HMV, Procter & Gamble, the NHS and KPMG have chosen to put staff through AAT qualifications. There are no formal entry requirements, although you will need to be numerate and literate. The vocational diploma and NVQ (SVQ in Scotland) routes to AAT qualification both afford relevant, practical training.

The NVQ (like all NVQs) is assessed on demonstrated competencies and has three stages, although with an accountancy degree you go straight to technician stage and relevant A levels and HNDs can mean you get exemptions as well:

1. Foundation – NVQ level 2 in Accounting

2. Intermediate – NVQ level 3 in Accounting

3. Technician – NVQ level 4 in Accounting.

It helps to be working in finance while studying, because this provides you with the necessary year's work experience and evidence of competencies for technician status.

If you are not able to demonstrate relevant competencies in the workplace, the diploma route will be more appropriate. This also has three stages, all of which need to be completed for technician status:

1. Foundation – certificate in accounting

2. Intermediate – advanced certificate in accounting

3. Technician – diploma in accounting.

There are 400 UK training centres which set their own course fees (approximately £400 to 800 per level). Additionally, AAT registration is £33 and examinations cost £30 to £35. Courses are run in a classroom setting, part time and by distance learning.

Profile: AAT

The history of accountancy goes back thousands of years to the days of Babylon and Assyria, where primitive accounting methods were used to record the growth of crops and herds.

While nowadays the practice may be more sophisticated, it still relies on the same essential principles – and from newsagents to multinational investment banks, it remains integral to running a successful business.

In short, the role of an accountant is, to report, record and analyse the financial transactions of a business. It is often referred to as 'the language of business' and, as such, accounting skills are highly sought after – even in a recession. This is shown in figures from last year,when, despite the economic downturn, accounting vacancies increased by 11%. Why is this? Well, as long as there is money in the world there will be a demand for accountants. It's fair to say it is one of the few recession-proof careers.

So how do I start a career in accountancy?

Vocational qualifications like the AAT Accounting Qualification provide a great starting point to anyone looking for a career in accountancy. The qualification is split into three levels (all recognised as qualifications in their own right) and students are taught all the way from basic costing principles to complex management accounting tasks. AAT's competence-based assessments mean students are taught to understand both the theory behind accounting and the practical application of that theory. This firm emphasis on work-based skills makes the qualification highly regarded by employers in a variety of sectors.

Case study

After choosing the AAT pathway into an accountancy career instead of university, Maddison Grant has never looked back.

"I first heard about AAT when studying my A Levels. I'd always enjoyed Maths so accounting seemed a good career choice.

"I was scared of incurring large student debt and wanted a practical qualification that would give me the flexibility to work full time.

"AAT is exactly what I needed. It helped me find a job in credit control and also an employer who would support my studies financially.

"Choosing AAT over university was the best decision I've ever made. I've avoided debt, am gaining a recognised qualification, first-hand experience, and, best of all, been promised a pay rise once I've qualified!"

Maddison is not on her own. Thousands of students start this journey every year, either studying AAT at college or at home by distance learning. The flexible study options mean there are courses available to suit everyone. Importantly, you don't need to be employed in accounting or have any previous experience to start, and there may even be funding available to help you with the tuition fees. Many students, like Maddison, find employment whilst they are studying, and if you're in an accounts role already, check to see if your employer will sponsor you.

Visit www.aat.org.uk for more information on how to get started or call our student recruitment team on 0845 863 0802. With more and more employers turning to apprenticeships and vocational qualifications – not to mention the rise in university fees – there really is no better time to get started.

The ACCA's CAT (Certified Accounting Technician) scheme www.accaglobal.com

Again combining study and practical experience (completed before, simultaneously or after), the CAT scheme is divided into beginner, intermediate and advanced levels and involves study towards nine papers, plus an online professionalism and ethics paper.

Open to all ages, it generally takes one to two years, but there is no time limit. No formal qualifications are required, although you will need reasonable literacy and numeracy. You could get started as a junior accounts clerk from as young as 16 years and you may be able to secure training as a modern apprentice. On passing, you would automatically transfer to the ACCA qualification.

Mature students

It is never too late! Just because you did not join that throng of competitive, driven and bright young people clambering for places in big accountancy firms on leaving university, does not mean that you could not have a go further down the line.

In a recent survey, *Accountancy* magazine found the average oldest trainee in the top 60 accountancy firms (data from 43 practices was available) to be 35 years, with one firm having a trainee aged 50. Results are shown in the table on p189.

Profile: Eagle Education

eagle
education & training ltd

We're here to help you succeed

We're a leading, successful distance learning provider approved by the Association of Accounting Technicians (AAT) and the International Association of Book-keepers (IAB). We specialise in providing distance learning courses for those who want to improve their career prospects and earning potential in the field of manual and computerised bookkeeping, accounting and payroll. Our specialism enables us to provide you with the best service and learning tools so you can obtain the best results!

Our students love our distance learning courses because we:

- Employ people to support you who have extensive accounting and business experience. They're excited to share your achievements.

- Create learning tools that are most suitable for distance learners. They're very enjoyable to use, keeping you interested and motivated.

- Respect traditional learning methods and embrace modern technologies. Students highly recommend our paper-based 'Study Buddy' and our interactive e-learning.

- Provide an efficient, friendly service that meets the expectations of our customers.

Many of our distance learning students are progressing rapidly, obtaining impressive exam results and enjoying successful careers!

The director is an *Accountancy Age* award winner

The judges particularly commented on the quality of eagle's learning resources, saying: "The Study Buddy system has made the daunting task of qualification markedly easier by engaging students in enjoyable, varied activities, enabling them to learn easily in manageable sections."

AccountancyAge
AWARDS
2 0 0 9
WINNER

Visit us online: www.eagle-education.co.uk
Or call us for a chat: +44 (0)1978 722511
Sample our course materials online today!

Case study

Elaine Humphries, Bookkeeper

"I can't describe how much of an achievement it feels to be able to pass AAT exams and be on a new career path, having been out of the education system for so long!"

After being made redundant for the fourth time, Elaine took the opportunity to change her career:

"Following redundancy, the Welsh Assembly provided retraining funding. I chose to study the Association of Accounting technicians' qualification at home as the most flexible option, so that I could look for new employment, whilst working towards the diploma."

Elaine finds the qualification interesting and challenging

"I have been pleasantly surprised to find just how much of the course relates to work I have done in the past. There is also quite a lot which is new to me, and it keeps me interested and challenged. I sat computer-based examinations. Passing my first exam – the first I have sat in 17 years – was a thrill and a great incentive to continue studying."

She has thoroughly enjoyed using eagle's unique study materials

"Whilst the textbooks are good, eagle's specially written Study Buddy presents each topic in a logical order and in bite-sized chunks, making new topics clear and much easier to understand. This is backed up by on-line tutorials, which reinforce learning."

Our exam tips work wonders

"I couldn't remember a ratio equation. However, I remembered the Study Buddy saying that you could be asked anything in the exam and that it was a question of working through the logic. That kept me going and logic prevailed!"

Our personal support is highly valued

"My personal tutor and her colleagues have been very helpful in providing detailed answers when I have not understood a topic properly. They have also given me informative and constructive feedback from mock exams. My tutor has kept pushing me in a very gentle and diplomatic manner so that I keep to the timetable we established and get the maximum out of my funding."

*"All in all, the learning experience with **eagle education** is very positive, sometimes challenging, but extremely rewarding."*

Visit us online: www.eagle.education.co.uk
Or call us for a chat: +44 (0)1978 722511
Sample our course materials online today!

TABLE 18: The ages of the oldest accountancy trainees in top firms

Age of oldest trainee in Top 60 firms	Number of firms
20–24 years	1
25–29 years	10
30–34 years	12
35–39 years	12
40–44 years	3
45–49 years	4
50–54 years	1
Total	43

PwC's Inspired Talent programme was discussed on p133. Perhaps you have excelled in a sporting field, made your first million pounds at the age of 16, or raised enormous amounts of money for charity? Perhaps you were the youngest person to cross the Channel on a raft or to play the harp in the Royal Albert Hall? Such achievements demonstrate commitment, determination, dedication, competitive spirit, and a desire to work hard and to win and meet goals. Employers recognise that not everyone can play rugby for England and still have the time to gain straight A grades in their examinations, and they may make concessions for people with such notable talent and grit. Indeed, firms might even relish the opportunity to bask in the reflected glory of a celebrity of sorts (they will employ successful sportspeople and adventurers but release them for meetings, expeditions and events).

Naturally, you do not have to be a star or academic to gain mature entry. You can train on the job, and the fact that CIMA, CIPFA and AAT do not set out stringent formal entry requirements mean that accountancy can be a viable option for a career change. Of course, we may all be needing to work into our seventies and beyond, given limited pension resources, and this, together with better health and longevity, and legislation against ageism, means that there are more opportunities for mature applicants. Should you be mature, you will obviously benefit from greater experience, and maybe better developed people and communication skills, more ability to handle responsibility, and greater focus, commitment and prudence.

ACCA has a Mature Student Entry Route (MSER) for those over 21 years and unable to enter via the professional examination route because they fail to meet the academic requirements. The only stipulation is that you must complete and pass the first two papers within two years.

Sponsorship for accountancy degrees

As discussed in chapter 3 (p135), many university degrees provide eligibility for exemptions from professional accountancy qualifications, and conversely, successful completion of ACCA qualifications provides automatic eligibility for an Oxford Brookes degree, (with just an additional 'Research and Analysis' project). Additionally, several firms and professional bodies are in partnership with particular universities to create salaried or sponsored programmes tailored toward the professional syllabus and providing valuable work placements.

University partnership programmes

The **ICAEW**, for example, has partnered with several universities to form practical and theoretical courses working toward **ACA** qualification. The year-long, salaried work placement counts as part of the ACA training contract, so post-degree qualification will take you two rather than three years.

Cardiff University

BSc Accounting (UCAS code: N400) www.cardiff.ac.uk/carbs/programmes/ ugrad/accounting.html

BSc Accounting and Finance (UCAS code: N490) www.cardiff.ac.uk/carbs/ programmes/ugrad/accfin.html

Manchester Business School

BSc Accounting (UCAS code: N400) www.mbs.ac.uk/programmes/undergraduate/ courses/accounting

Warwick Business School

BSc Accounting and Finance (UCAS code: NN34) www.wbs.ac.uk/students/
undergraduate/accounting-finance

PwC has partnered with two academic institutions, which offer four-year sandwich
degrees, including study towards **ACA** qualification and three paid work placements
(earning at least £20,000). Successful completion of these theoretical and practical
courses even guarantees a job offer from PwC.

PwC and Henley Business School at University of Reading

Four-year BA Accounting and Business degree (UCAS code: NN41) www.henley.
reading.ac.uk/pwc

PwC and Newcastle University

Four-year BA Business Accounting and Finance degree (UCAS code: NN14) www.ncl.
ac.uk/flyingstart

Ernst & Young is in partnership with **Lancaster University Business School**, to
support and run a similar Institute of Chartered Accountants of Scotland (ICAS)
fast-track, sandwich degree course in BSc Accounting, Auditing and Finance,
including up to 18 months' paid employment. www.lums.lancs.ac.uk/departments/
accounting/undergraduate/eydegree

Degree sponsorship

KPMG, **ICAS** and **Durham University Business School** have also, in principle,
agreed a School Leavers programme (extending to **Exeter** and **Birmingham**)
which will involve sponsorship for the four-year degree element and salaried
employment throughout (starting on £20,000 in London). www.kpmgcareers.
co.uk/A-LevelTrainees/default.aspx?pg=1603

Teach First

Certain employers, for example PwC and P&G, have partnered with the Teach First charity. Teach First is an initiative to encourage the highest-calibre graduates to defer the start of their career, and to work as a salaried teacher for two years first in a challenging school.

Should you be accepted on the scheme, you might feel that you are contributing in a positive way and giving something back, through acting as change agents and inspirational role models for educationally disadvantaged pupils. But also, employers recognise the benefit of such intensive leadership training for you personally, in terms of enhanced people skills, communication, influencing, presentation, planning and organisational skills. Obviously, the charity's hope is that such graduates, who might never have considered a career in teaching, will remain in the field and carve out successful careers, or at least remain actively involved in an ambassadorial capacity.

You have to be successful in applications to both Teach First and the partner employer to secure a place on the scheme.

See http://graduates.teachfirst.org.uk for more information.

6

Work experience and internships

"Did you ever hear of a kid playing accountant – even if they wanted to be one?"

Jackie Mason

Why are work experience and internships important?

Increasingly, accountancy recruiters are looking not just for exceptional academic achievement, but also for substantial work experience and commercial awareness. Many students are taking relevant gap year and vacation internships not just to gain a better understanding of the work and their feelings toward it, but also to add weight to a CV. With 45 applications for each position in chartered accountancy, it is estimated that about one third will have worked for the employer previously.

Some accountancy and business sandwich degree courses offer placement opportunities, and the university may find these for you, but you should also consider sourcing some holiday internships in accountancy yourself. If you are not on a sandwich course, or if you are on an unrelated degree course, you will certainly need to locate your own opportunities, in order to increase your post-degree credibility, marketability and knowledge base. Internships often lead to job offers as well, so you may gain a permanent position should you sufficiently impress.

Accountancy internships range from a year-long 'thick' sandwich placement or several six-week 'thin' placements, during academic courses, to salaried vacation work throughout a degree course or during the long summer breaks. They may also be taken before or after a degree and usually involve supervised practical training. Some opportunities roll all year round, but most require early application in December or January for the following summer.

While big-name firms can add weight to your CV, experience with smaller firms can also be valuable, and is perhaps more likely to result in your obtaining an 'in through the back door' job offer. Contact your local high street practices and the finance departments of small companies in your area, besides the obvious blue chips.

Benefits of internships

- You can explore career opportunities, consider which specialisms hold greatest appeal and learn how a firm works.

- You can network and build positive relationships which could serve you well in the future.

- You might find a mentor to encourage, advise and inspire you.

- You should earn some cash! Other than when volunteering with charities, which are exempt, or if working for under a year as an obligatory part of an academic course, or if below school leaving age, or if simply 'shadowing' someone, you should be entitled to at least the minimum wage.

- You should gain valuable skills, knowledge and experience, perhaps learning people, communication and leadership skills, as well as developing technical competencies and putting theory into practice.

- You will learn about the disciplines of business, and the work experience could even count towards the practical experience requirement (PER) element of your professional training.

How to find internships

As ever, it is not what you know but who you know. Personal contacts are still one of the best ways of creating opportunities. Who do you or your relatives know working in accountancy? Could they put in a good word or offer you some work in the holidays (paid or otherwise)?

Locate local firms and those of interest (e.g. through the local Chamber of Commerce or Business Link, Yellow Pages, or online sources like www. careersineurope.hobsons.com). Apply speculatively, highlighting relevant talents and motivations and throwing in a reason for particularly wanting experience in that firm (you may need to do some research on the number of employees and offices, the main type of work, specialism or business, global locations, and recent events, restructuring and deals).

Look on accountancy firms' websites. Many have officially organised internships for which you might apply, and many of these are tailored toward different academic levels and stages.

Scan the blue chips' websites. Procter & Gamble offer a finance and accounting internship for students in their penultimate or final year of study.

The professional bodies' websites (CIMA, ACCA, ICAEW) may sometimes advertise internships on the jobs pages:

- http://trainingvacancies.icaew.com/jobboard

- www.cipfa.org.uk/students/prospective/vacancies.cfm

As always, a simple internet search on 'accountancy internships' throws up a number of starting points. There are websites devoted to internships, perhaps abroad, (e.g. www.internoptions.com), and also recruitment websites which list vacancies (e.g. www.targetjobs.co.uk graduate jobs and careers advice – click on 'work experience'; www.allaboutcareers.com graduate advice, jobs, internships and placements; www.milkround.com click on 'jobs and internships'). Other helpful sites include:

- www.insidecareers.co.uk

- www.ratemyplacement.co.uk

- www.prospects.ac.uk

The university careers office should additionally have relationships with employers and alumni, which you might exploit.

Applying for internships

Covering letters

Covering letters should follow a simple format and should be concise and to the point, flagging why you should be considered. Keep it brief and don't be afraid to use bullet points.

- Initial paragraph: set the scene as to why you are writing.

- Middle paragraphs: detail your unique selling points and what you have to offer.

- Final paragraph: give a conclusion, explaining how you intend to follow up.

Initial paragraph

Explain where you have seen the advertisement for an intern, which mutual contact has suggested you apply to that firm, or why you have personally chosen to approach that particular company or practice. Make clear that you are seeking a work placement or salaried internship (in the accounts department, if not approaching a professional practice) and which dates suit you best.

Middle paragraph

Obviously, your CV should highlight your qualifications, achievements and skills, but take this opportunity to flag relevant selling points – what do *you* have to offer *them*? As with all applications, the busy reader tends to be looking for reasons not to shortlist you, so you need a brief, compelling argument and hard evidence that you would be particularly competent and committed as an accountancy intern.

Clearly, you are not likely to have a great deal of work experience at this stage, so you may need to mention leisure and voluntary achievements and responsibilities. In particular, as with the CV, provide examples of where you have been promoted, elected, praised or rewarded, showing that peers and superiors recognised your talents. Being elected as head girl at school suggests popularity, responsibility, organisational, people and communication skills; being a treasurer for the winning team in Young Enterprise highlights analytical and numerical strengths. Some examples may be more general: 'selected to play for England' could evidence drive, team play, fitness and energy.

Final paragraph

In the last paragraph, you should summarise, reiterate enthusiasm, and discuss follow-up. Say something like: 'I will telephone in one week to discuss how we might progress this request.' This call will allow you to ensure that the application has been safely received; to ask pertinent, probing questions which reflect favourably on you; to direct attention to your own particular application; and to enable you to become a 'real person' in the eyes of the company, and therefore rather harder to reject than an impersonal, unknown applicant.

Even if you are not successful in securing an accountancy internship on this occasion, it can be politic to send a letter thanking them for their consideration, expressing disappointment, but continued enthusiasm and the hope that they will view you more favourably next time!

Making the most of an internship

Beforehand

- Do your homework about the firm, so that you do not appear too naïve. Look on the website and at economic and industry news in trade magazines and newspapers.

- Consider what you want from the placement – contacts, understanding, personal development . . . a job?

- What is the dress code? You could stand outside and watch people coming in and out, but it may be simpler just to telephone and ask!

During

- Try to make a good first impression: this lasts. Arrive early, take notes (if only of names), ask questions, build positive relationships, listen patiently and look interested.

- Do not pretend to understand when you do not: better to check, ask for repeat instructions and clarification, and to admit that you do not get it, or understand what is expected, rather than to mess up. Indeed, people may even respect you more if prepared to admit that you do not understand.

- Prioritise and show initiative.

- Volunteer for additional tasks and responsibilities, in order to raise your profile, look keen and develop personally, and don't act as though making coffee is beneath you.

- Always do the best you can and ask for regular feedback meetings, which will mean the boss has to monitor and really take notice of what you are doing, as well as enabling you to correct anything which you may be doing less well.

- Be diplomatic and make friends, not enemies: you may be coming back as a trainee accountant in due course.

- Speak up: if you have a good idea or can see that something might be done differently or better, make a suggestion.

- Be professional in both dress and attitude: be on time, do not make personal phone calls, take work seriously, and don't go in with a hangover.

- Have fun: demonstrating that you enjoy the work in accountancy, and that you fit in.

Afterwards

- Request a reference, or enlist your boss as a referee for the future.

- Keep a log of what you did and learned (you may be able to detail this for your PER), and perhaps what you would or should have done differently.

- Write a letter of thanks: one accountant was once offered a job subsequently because he had been the only intern to have done so! This is an opportunity to praise the boss and the team for their input, leadership, sharing of knowledge and support, but also to remind them of what you were able to contribute, by expressing your gratitude for having been afforded that opportunity. State that the experience has made you even more enthusiastic about an accountancy career. Of course, your letter will also provide prompts and an *aide-mémoire* for the experience and achievements you would like them to mention in their reference.

How to write a CV

What does your CV really say about you?

Everyone will tell you to write a CV differently! There is no definitive, right way of writing one, any more than there is only one way of presenting a company brochure or writing a report, but you do need to remember that this is your personal self-marketing document, targeted at an audience of accountancy recruiters.

Initially, you should think about what you have to offer the firm; as with application forms and interviews, you need to highlight relevant skills and competencies (such as numeracy, time management, people skills, IT, team working and communication), showing that you can do the job and that you will fit in. This will involve some self-assessment and consideration of which skills and personal qualities match accountancy and perhaps that specialism or sector, in particular. You are the person who knows your achievements and experience best, so you are the best person to write the CV – if you need someone to check over the grammar and spelling later, then fine, but try to write it yourself. This should also enable you to be more prepared for the interview and even to build your confidence as you start to recall and 'big up' successes which you had previously forgotten or dismissed.

Do not simply list your responsibilities in previous jobs; the reader will have some idea of what was involved from the job title. A potential employer wants to know that you were good, that you made a difference, that you were successful, so provide hard evidence. Instead of 'responsible for dealing with incoming calls', write 'commended for rapid and efficient handling of incoming calls'; instead of 'general administrative duties', describe how you 'initiated the streamlining of all administrative processes to reduce duplication and paper'.

First, make a list of all your previous jobs, courses and qualifications by date and establishment, and take note of any awards, promotions, nominations, commendations or accolades, which you may have received for each.

Second, carefully consider the skills, experience, competencies and qualifications required for this post or internship – these should be clearly outlined in the job and person specifications. Look at your first list and note where you can draw out real evidence and examples of relevant achievements and contributions, highlighting these competencies.

Do not simply write, say, 'strong communication and people skills' without providing concrete examples and corroborative evidence, drawn from study, work and leisure, to substantiate your claim. Leadership skills, for instance, could be illustrated by your having chaired a Young Enterprise initiative (especially if you won!). Communication skills could be demonstrated through success in debating with the Model United Nations, through winning a poetry competition or contributing to the university newspaper. Analytical skills might be highlighted by your having been the local schools chess champion. Strong time management could be reflected in juggling four A levels, while working part time and representing England in hockey!

Pressure management could be proven through your having calmly dealt with being mugged and having your passport stolen during your gap year. Determination and grit may be shown through Duke of Edinburgh expeditions. Obviously, your work experience will be limited, so you will need to draw from all aspects of life and any previous positions, even if not obviously pertinent to accountancy (although the more relevant commercial or financial experience and internships you are able to mention, the better).

In particular, recruiters will want to see evidence of problem solving and analysis (research for your undergraduate dissertation?), numeracy (statistical or mathematical qualifications), teamwork (theatre or sport?), commercial awareness (Saturday job, internships, buying and selling on eBay?), interpersonal skills (elected head girl, head boy or student representative?), and organisational and time management ability (working to deadlines?).

A CV creates the first impression for a recruiter, who is probably inundated with applications and looking for reasons to discard your application, rather than to select it during the initial sort. The CV is your personal brochure, so do not detail the bad points of the product. Do not mention, for instance, that retaken year at university: not only might you eliminate yourself at first base, but an interviewer may subsequently focus on that and waste valuable time discussing a negative, rather than an achievement. It is permissible to omit the negative, but your CV must not be a work of fiction.

A CV should:

- sell you and highlight value to the accounts department or practice

- provide structure and discussion points for an interview

- leave the interviewer with a written record of how you match the person specification.

Hit them straight off with compelling and impressive information which hooks them in. You may have only 60 seconds to put your message across to the recruiter, so you must immediately capture their attention and interest. Leave any bad news to the end and place it on the right of the page (poor grades, for instance, which it may be better to leave out altogether). Personal details are not selling points, so leave those to the end too. Whatever your marital status, your age or the ages of your children, or your nationality, someone could read something into it, so omit these altogether. Similarly, do not waste selling space listing referees; if needed, they will ask.

There is no need to write 'Curriculum Vitae' on the document, either; the reader should be able to see what it is. Just head the page with a name in a large bold font (a statement of confidence) and, centred underneath, your address and contact details in small type.

Start with a summary or personal profile of up to 30 words, demonstrating skills, attitudes, knowledge and experience (SAKE), and stating your career objective. This is your personal banner, conditioning the reader to anticipate positive and relevant information. What follows must justify this statement. For example: 'Effective, ambitious, personable and professional graduate engineer, with significant vacation experience in finance (both in practice and industry), seeking to capitalise on people, quantitative, analytical, communication and organisational skills in chartered accountancy.'

Write in the past tense and use punchy, positive impact, action words, which create an image of a concrete achievement, something done... completed... won. Say 'negotiated' rather than 'liaised', and 'controlled' rather than 'I was responsible for'. Where possible, avoid other passive or reactive words, such as supported, rejected, provided, prepared, maintained, or rectified, although these can have their place. Rather than 'work experience', write 'career achievements to date', suggesting plenty more successes to come.

When listing jobs, what you did, with whom, and when, list the job title on the left, the organisation (no address) in the centre, and then the dates. When describing achievements, think SAY (situation, action, yield). Do not simply state responsibilities, but provide evidence to quantify and demonstrate success and prove your claims. 'I was responsible for dealing with customers and stocktaking' creates a far less favourable impression than 'Promoted to supervisory role. Consistently top salesperson. Ensured attractive and compelling merchandising to draw in customers and boost sales of less popular lines. Streamlined stocktaking processes, greatly improving efficiency and control'.

Think! What was the positive result of your action or intervention? Try asking 'So what?' after everything you write. 'Devised a new spreadsheet.' So what? 'Well, the company thought it was so good they used it across the firm.' Or 'Well, it reduced the time needed to complete that task by half.'

It is not essential to list your interests outside work, but it can be useful in painting a more detailed picture of you as a person. Sporting interests can imply an active, fit, energetic constitution. Chess or crossword puzzles could conjure up 'logical, intelligent, precise, problem solver' in the reader's mind. Captain of rugby team could imply sociability, team-player or organisational skills. Rather than simply 'reading', you might add detail: especially the *Financial Times* and autobiographies of modern entrepreneurs. Think of the different images someone might have of a person interested in amateur dramatics, against one listing trainspotting as a hobby. However, do ensure that you have some knowledge and experience of the pursuits you put down.

Reference to salary is also best avoided on a CV. Indeed, such discussions are best left as late as possible in negotiations – although this may not be possible if a recruitment agency is involved.

Presentation

Your presentation of the document will obviously be very important. Here are some tips.

- Use plain, white, good-quality A4 paper.

- The margin at the bottom should be larger than that at the top and sides, and blocks of script should be balanced centrally.

- Right-hand justification may give the impression of a mass-produced document, so it may be advisable to avoid this.

- Remember also that a spellchecker will not necessarily pick up typographic errors, so proofread thoroughly. No one wants an accountant who is not good with detail.

Having gone through the self-assessment process and emphasised your strengths on a CV, you will no doubt find that your confidence increases. You should find that you have done and achieved more than you thought and you should have clear evidence that you have a great deal to offer to a future employer and that you would make a great accountant. Writing that dreaded CV can make you feel really good about yourself. If you have already sent a CV, but now feel that this does not do you justice, simply send another, saying that you are forwarding an updated version for their records.

7

Finding your first training role

Whichever route you choose to go down – whether it's a Training Contract, or perhaps AAT or CAT qualification, or straight from school – this chapter will give you the tools you need to get onto your chosen path. At this stage, you will have undertaken internships and involved yourself in a host of extracurricular activities to add weight to your CV, and you will have done your research into the firms, sectors, qualifications and roles in accountancy to decide what types of roles you want to apply for. In this chapter, we will help you locate opportunities to apply for, and then give you the tools and advice you need to secure the role.

Locating opportunities

How do you actually find jobs to apply for? It is very easy to fall into the trap of simply looking for advertised vacancies, but if you are applying for that job, no doubt so are another 300 people and you are suddenly competing with all these other candidates. It can be easier to slip quietly through the back door through personal contacts, although sometimes this means that you are making less of an active choice about where you want to work, or in which specialism or role.

Of course, there are also recruitment agencies to do some of the work for you (although these may be gatekeepers, looking for reasons to discard you in the shortlisting, rather than people who can actually give you the job), and direct applications are also worth a try, whether a speculative approach or a formal application through the company website.

The important thing in this difficult and competitive economic climate is to have a balanced self-marketing campaign, exploiting all the approaches we'll give you later in this chapter.

For major firms, go to their websites and search for vacancies and training roles. Some recruit all year round, whereas others have one or two set times per year for accepting applications, for example September and June campaigns.

University careers service

The university careers offices forge valuable links with local and national employers, and some have databases for networking with alumni who are willing to provide help, advice and information. The university (and indeed the local careers service) has job boards which list vacancies. Companies are becoming more community-focused, which means that they increasingly advertise locally.

Graduate recruitment fairs and events

Graduate fairs are good starting points for contacts and information, and it is always worth taking copies of your CV to leave with exhibitors – you could even end up with a job!

While this is not an interview, you do want to make a good impression so that the recruiter is keen on hearing from you again. Dress smartly, not formally. Take a name so that you can write afterwards, expressing enthusiasm and thanking the recruiter for their time, help and advice.

Speaking with graduate recruiters can be valuable, both to learn what they are looking for and to practise your self-marketing skills. Do not speak exclusively with accountancy firms – remember that blue chips also have accountancy trainees on their graduate training schemes (finance stream) and you should take this opportunity to explore the differences and your feelings towards the different sectors. Make sure you know your talents, strengths and selling points (what competencies do they value?), and put these across succinctly. Prepare as you would for an interview.

Often, there are recent graduate employees on site to quiz and to tell you about their experiences and the firm's culture. Obviously this is bound to be positive, but you may gain some insights, and as stated previously, one man's meat is another's poison. Have some questions pre-prepared and arrive early so that you have quality time with recruiters and stand out, rather than being lost in the masses when the rush starts. The research and information gained may also come in valuable during the selection process. If nothing else, you are likely to leave with a bag of freebies!

Lists of such events may be found listed on sites such as www.swat.co.uk, www.milkround.com or www.gradjobs.co.uk. A comprehensive list of fairs is also listed on the Prospects website (www.prospects.ac.uk). An events calendar for chartered accountancy may be found on www.insidecareers.co.uk.

Milk round

The term 'milk round' was coined in the 1960s and refers to the practice of recruiters 'doing the rounds' and touring the country to present at graduate fairs and entice the students to join their graduate training schemes. Such tours traditionally occur in the autumn and summer terms and are organised individually with university careers services.

Milk round activities have increasingly moved online, thus providing wider access to target groups, and benefitting both students and recruiters. Web-based graduate job boards enable you to compare different schemes, to upload your CV and to apply for specific jobs. See www.milkround.com for more information.

Internet searches

There are so many ways of using the internet in a job search these days, from looking directly at the websites of companies, to looking at newspaper advertisements online, to scanning the professional bodies' websites for jobs, to locating or viewing advertised vacancies with general and traditional recruitment agencies and job sites, to perusing specialist graduate careers sites with jobs sections.

Traditional recruitment agencies

Vacancies may be found on general recruitment agency sites like www.reed.co.uk; www.michaelpage.co.uk; www.ambition.co.uk and www.hays.co.uk – simply search in the 'finance and accountancy' sections using keywords such as 'trainee accountant', 'trainee' or 'finance trainee'.

Financial recruitment agencies

There are also specialist financial recruitment agencies, such as www.roberthalf.co.uk; www.rkaccountancy.co.uk; www.cameronwallace.com; www.markssattin.co.uk; www.greenwellgleeson.co.uk, but some may only deal with qualified or part-qualified accountants. SWATuk (www.swat.co.uk) recruits for several of the top 50 firms of, mostly London-based, Chartered Accountants.

Financial job sites

Some online job sites are dedicated to finance. You might upload your CV for recruiters to find, or reply to advertised vacancies:

- www.gaapweb.com

- www.totallyfinancial.com

- www.accountancyagejobs.com

- www.accountancyjobsonline.co.uk

Graduate job sites

Some job sites specialise in graduate opportunities:

- www.gradjobs.co.uk

Media advertisements

Newspaper advertisements may obviously also be found online. Should none of the listed positions seem quite right, through looking at which agencies are advertising, you might identify those to whom you might send your CV for future reference:

- http://jobs.guardian.co.uk

- http://jobs.independent.co.uk

- http://jobs.thetimes.co.uk

Social networking sites

This is the internet age – look on LinkedIn and Facebook for positions and contacts. LinkedIn has various groups that you might join to network, and many target companies will now have Facebook fan pages to help you gain insights into the firm and to learn when their next recruitment campaign will start. Companies sometimes even advertise specific vacancies.

Specialist public sector job sites

For CIPFA opportunities, you might look at specialist public sector jobs sites like:

- www.jobsgopublic.com

- www.publicsectorjobs.net

- www.lgjobs.com

- www.jobs.nhs.uk

- www.pfjobs.co.uk

Professional bodies' job pages

The professional bodies do list some vacancies on their jobs pages:

- http://myjobs.cimaglobal.com

- www2.accaglobal.com

- www.icaewjobs.com

- www.cipfarecruitment.org.uk

Directories

These can be valuable for speculative applications as well as for identifying graduate management training schemes in finance and accountancy.

Previously Hobson's Directory, Targetjobs lists employers from A to Z and provides comprehensive details of graduate training schemes: http://targetjobs.co.uk.

The Milkround website also has an A–Z directory of graduate employers: www.milkround.com/employers/directory.

The Times publishes an annual guide to the 100 Best Graduate Employers: www.top100graduateemployers.com.

Contacts

Never assume that you do not know anyone who could help. Perhaps your neighbour's daughter heads up an accounts department? Perhaps your boyfriend's uncle is a senior partner with loads of contacts in the profession?

Never ask for a job directly: simply ask for information and help. Leave a CV 'in case they should hear of anything', and never leave or hang up until you have several other names whom you might contact next. Do not forget to send a thank-you email, which can sometimes prompt them to remember someone else, or to think of an additional way they might help.

Accountancy trade magazines

These may be valuable for recruitment pages, or simply to identify which companies are in the news and potentially recruiting. Of course, reading these will also help with your general knowledge for interviews:

- www.accountancymagazine.com

- www.accountancyage.com

- www2.accaglobal.com

- www.camagonline.co.uk

- www.accountingweb.co.uk

Apply early

Once you have found positions to apply for, it's crucial that you apply for your chosen position in good time. You also need to leave a fair amount of time for completing application forms and application processes which in themselves are lengthy, in-depth and multi-stage. Early applications may be pushed through more quickly with less of a backlog, potentially speeding up the process as well.

Training and recruitment mistakes are costly, so to safeguard you, your potential colleagues and indeed potential clients, the selection procedure is very rigorous. Employers need to know that you have the ability, motivation and personal qualities to do the job and to fit in. The thorough selection process often involves several stages, and more than likely will include:

- an application form

- online psychometric measures (often repeated later to prove that it was really you who took the test)

- an initial sifting interview (and/or telephone pre-screening)

- a competency-based interview

- a day at an assessment centre.

Application forms

Large firms are increasingly using application forms instead of CVs to sift and sort applicants. CVs in all their formats can be very varied and candidates may be hard to compare. Not everyone's CV does them full justice or tells the recruiter what they really want to know (even if a suitably tailored CV should). Application forms are specifically designed to give everyone an equal chance, enabling you to sell yourself and to fully demonstrate the desired competencies. They generally cover education (do not lie or stretch the truth – they check, and integrity is a fundamental requirement for accountancy), career motivation, positions of responsibility and work experience (some firms insist on at least four weeks of work experience, not necessarily paid or continuous). They ask you to provide situational, behavioural examples, demonstrating key competencies required for the job.

In most cases these days, the application form is online, but it may not need to be completed all in one sitting; you can usually save drafts and return to the form later. This is always a good idea, because you might then spot previously unnoticed errors and think up additional or better things to say! Of course, you do not want to agonise forever over this form, but you do need to ensure that it does you justice and makes you sufficiently attractive to call for the next stage (the initial online psychometric measures). Be concise, because you can elaborate at interview. It pays to have someone else check it over for typos and grammatical errors. If you do cut and paste between application forms, make sure the copy is not overtly tailored toward a competitor, and do not simply repeat statements which you have read in the website or brochure!

Always remember to proofread your application

Real mistakes found on applications for accountancy positions

- 'I was closely involved in every aspect of my former company, right up to its bankruptcy.'

- 'Developed and recommended an annual operating expense fudget.'

- 'Proven ability to track down and correct erors.'

- 'Instrumental in ruining an entire operation for a chain operator.'

Source: University of Kent Careers Advisory Service website

You may already have examples documented on your CV, but you should certainly prepare several for the interview stages to enable you to present hard evidence that you are able to deal with conflict, organise and be self-disciplined, solve problems and work well in a team. What was the situation, what action did you take and how did you behave, and what was the outcome (make sure this was positive)? Obviously, you will need to draw examples from personal, leisure, academic and university life, because, unless a career-changer, you are unlikely to have a great deal of work experience. Keep a copy of your application form for future reference (although this can often still be accessed online).

Elements of employability

PwC has a useful 'Employability Guide' which will help you identify and highlight those selling points, qualities and competencies which are valued. These fall under 10 categories:

1. coach and develop yourself and others

2. communicate with impact and empathy

3. be curious: learn, share and innovate

4. lead and reinforce team success

5. build and maintain relationships

6. show you have courage and integrity

7. manage projects and money

8. be open-minded, practical and quick to adapt

9. build and use commercial and technical know-how

10. caring about client service.

By ensuring the content of your application fits clearly within one of these categories, you will be creating a well-structured and focused application.

Answers to common questions

To show that you know what you are in for should you be successful, questions which may appear on an application form include the following.

Please provide us with your understanding of the professional services offered by the firm and in particular, the work undertaken in your chosen line of service (maximum 150 words).

Mention drive, commitment, ambition and striving for excellence. Discuss professional training and skills, and dealing with and helping clients. Throw in analytical and problem solving skills and rising to a challenge. For audit, include words like 'true and fair' representation, and 'legal requirement'. Emphasise how you might be helping companies to stay buoyant in the marketplace and appealing more to investors. You would not just be policing but also consulting and advising to remedy on weaknesses in processes and so on.

Why are you keen to work for this particular firm?

Obviously, this is difficult in Public Practice, because the Big Four firms all offer such great career prospects (a professional qualification, variety, teamwork, opportunity for progression, learning and responsibility, reputation, and scope for travel and secondments and so on).

You really need to be able to throw in some specific examples of why that firm may be better, or preferable to you.

- Perhaps it is bigger and more profitable?

- Perhaps it does more for charity or the community?

- Perhaps it has been voted best for disability, training, or women?

- Perhaps it is ranked higher as a graduate employer?

- Perhaps the study timetable is different, or the cultural climate of the firm more friendly, individualistic or dynamic?

- Does it have a stronger tax or audit department, or has it won awards for corporate finance?

- Maybe it has a higher profile for sustainability?

What research have you undertaken about this firm?

Some of the above answers will obviously demonstrate that you have done your research, but have some facts and figures ready! Do not just have a quick look the night before – study carefully and make notes. Scrutinise the website and brochures (corporate and careers), and find any recent mentions or articles in the press and financial media (press, TV and internet), which you might be able to casually drop into the conversation. Talk to people working in the field, especially for that firm, and look at professional bodies' websites to ensure that you are fully conversant with requirements for qualifications, and with industry news.

What do you see yourself doing in your first year here?

You must know this and be able to demonstrate that you know what you are applying for and why it is right for you. Try telephoning the firms and actually asking what you would be doing in the first and second years (other than, of course, studying very hard).

For audit, you might mention substantial travel and being out at clients' sites, taking part in audits, learning the ropes and taking increasing responsibility, meeting clients, networking and making new friends and contacts.

We are committed to providing our clients with exceptional services, which add value to their business. From a business perspective, which organisation would be your preferred client and what services do you think we would be providing to enhance the organisation's continued business success (maximum 150 words)?

There are clearly two parts to this. You need to demonstrate that you understand what makes a good business and what services the firm might offer to improve performance, such as taxation advice, strategy and performance consulting, and internal controls.

It may be preferable to choose a client that is not a current client, because the interviewer may be overly knowledgeable or sensitive. Avoid really technical businesses and perhaps even dotcoms, which may have business models less familiar to more mature recruiters. Select a business you and most others would know, such as a high street store.

Here are some additional questions you might face on the online application form.

- Describe an activity which took you out of your comfort zone.

- Detail an instance when you have had to motivate a team. Tell us about when you have applied your learning to make a real difference.

- Describe a situation when voluntarily you took responsibility and showed initiative.

- Outline an instance when you have had to put in sustained effort under difficult circumstances.

Psychometric tests

Psychometric tests are scientifically designed and validated measures, which aim to objectively assess reasoning potential and typical behaviour. You may well have already undertaken several cognitive attainment tests (CATs) at school, so they should not be too daunting; indeed, many people really enjoy the challenges and puzzles, especially when they are bright and confident in their intellectual capabilities.

All large accountancy firms will incorporate psychometric measures into their selection process, and there is likely to be an initial short online screening measure (which is reapplied later if you make it through), and further, more in-depth assessments later at assessment centre stage. Some accountancy firms send through the online tests within about two days of you submitting your application.

You should take time to work carefully through the practices for these online measures. Make sure that you are in a quiet space and will not be interrupted when completing the real test. More mature candidates, who grew up with pencils and paper, could potentially be less comfortable than the younger internet generation, who may hate to put pen to paper. Be well organised, with notepad, calculator, mouse and keyboard placed ergonomically, so that no time is wasted reaching past things to work out or mark an answer. The art is for you to go as quickly as you can without making silly mistakes. Try to relax, but don't be surprised if your heart races as you watch the on-screen timer ticking away as you race against the clock.

Aptitude measures

Aptitude measures are problems presented in different formats, which predict your potential for learning and reasoning through different channels. These might include words (verbal reasoning), numbers (numerical reasoning), or patterns (diagrammatic/perceptual, and sometimes logical reasoning). Aptitude measures are standardised to ensure that everyone has the same instructions and thus the same chance, and 'normed' to compare your results with the distribution curve of a particular population or group (such as graduates). They are timed and most people are not expected to reach the end, so do not panic, but work as quickly and accurately as possible.

Most aptitude tests are designed to measure innate potential rather than learned knowledge. Many of the accountancy assessments call for a good grasp of basic mathematics, though – reading tables and graphs, calculating percentages and ratios, currency conversions and time/date problems – so it is worth your brushing up on these. You may be allowed notepaper and a calculator. You will have some practice questions before the real thing, and there are a number of sites that enable you to have a go at some practice tests ahead of time (see box on p.218). Do ensure that you read each question carefully and that you understand what is required before committing yourself, because multiple choice answers may be similar and designed to include the most common errors.

Try to find out ahead of time which test house designs the aptitude tests, e.g. SHL or Cubik's, so that you know which kind to practise. The latter is said to be particularly difficult, with just 30% of candidates passing. One publication you might find helpful is *How to Pass Professional Level Psychometric Tests* (Kogan Page, 2010).

Firms will generally have a percentile cut-off point, so scores below this will automatically eliminate you. This can place perfectionists at risk, because they often work particularly slowly and carefully through such measures, answering most correctly but completing too few to score highly. It is important for you to find the correct balance between speed and accuracy.

Websites for practising psychometric tests

Jobtestprep: www.jobtestprep.co.uk/ernstyoung.aspx

Cubiks: http://practicetests.cubiks.com

Assessment Day: www.assessmentday.co.uk

Criterion Partnership: http://criterionpartnership.co.uk/psychometrics_help

The Morrisby Organisation: www.morrisby.com/content/candidates-support/faqs/sample-morrisby-profile-questions

Knight Chapman Psychological: www.kcpltd.com

Mr M W Lock CPsychol AFBPsS: www.formula4leadership.com/menu_questions.htm

Previsor (ASE): www.ase-solutions.co.uk/products/certifications

Psytech International: www.practicetests.co.uk

Saville Consulting UK: www.savilleconsulting.com/products/aptitude_preparationguides.aspx

SHL Group: www.shldirect.com

Team Focus: www.profilingforsuccess.com/products/profile_yo.php

Personality measures

These sample your usual behaviour or style, in order to predict how you are likely to behave in future situations. Firms rarely use results to eliminate applicants, but may use them as interview prompts to explore accuracy and potential concerns. These are self-perception questionnaires which may involve rating how much a behaviour is like you, or making a forced selection between several types of behaviour.

There are no right or wrong answers, but it may be worth your keeping in mind the main competencies and requirements of the job. Obviously you do not want to fib your way into a position – ultimately this will be good for no one if you are not suited to the work, so selection processes are to protect you as well – but nor should you be brutally honest about your weaker points. While questions may seem transparent, they are not always assessing what you may think. The question about whether 'I talk to strangers on the train' could be looking at unconventionality rather than sociability.

Psychometric tests must be interpreted by trained users. Some are 'normed' and your results compared with certain specified populations or groups – graduates, for instance, or women – whereas others are 'ipsative', which means they simply look at strengths of traits within the individual rather than compared with others. For example, are you rating analytical behaviour stronger than people-facing behaviour?

Your first response is usually the most accurate – if you think too long, you will find it harder to make a decision. That said, there is no time limit, and you should avoid rushing and should take some time to consider how your chosen behavioural preference looks in the light of the job requirements. Would, for instance, 'I like to do new things' or 'I prefer to be working with others' be a good or a bad thing in the role?

Sometimes, the choices are scenario-based, which can also give you some insight into what it is like working in the field.

Pre-screen (telephone) interview

Telephone interviews are common, as they take up less time for the interviewer. On the telephone, you should prepare and act as though the interview is face to face (so no sips of coffee or snacks). It should take 10 to 15 minutes.

- Be present and ready to take the call.

- Stand rather than remain seated, to remain alert and focused.

- Smile! Smiling can be 'sensed' by the interviewer and helps you relax.

- Ensure that you have done your research and that you have this and copies of your application form and CV to hand – not that you want to be heard shuffling through papers to find information, so make just one or two pages of notes which you can have open on the table.

- Make sure that you will not be interrupted by friends, family, dog or phones; shut the door in a quiet room with good mobile reception (or perhaps access to a landline on which you might be called back).

- If you cannot hear the question, ask the interviewer to repeat it rather than guess and waffle.

- Speak clearly, concisely and with enthusiasm.

- Don't feel you have to fill awkward silences by blurting something out.

Many of the questions will already have been covered on the application form, but you need to prepare and practise answers to possible questions. Ideally, you would have someone in the field act as interviewer, but a friend or relative could also role-play the interviewer. Even better if you could find someone who has been through the process with that firm and can provide some inside tips. Your aim is to communicate well and convey motivation.

Example questions

Describe a time you gave a presentation

Again, set the scene, describing what it was for. Explain how you went about researching and planning it, and what exactly you did and how you put your message across. Highlight that it was well received and, ideally, describe the positive outcome: you were offered the job, received a high mark, or won the business or competition.

When have you delivered an unpleasant message?

What was the situation? Why was it difficult to communicate – were you rejecting someone, conveying bad news, dealing with conflict or a sensitive issue? How did you plan and approach it? What did you say, do and feel? What was the (positive or at least acceptable) result?

Why this firm? Why audit (or whichever service line you have chosen)? What do you understand you will be doing in year one?

These have been considered above in the 'application forms' section.

What is your understanding of professional services/of this firm's services?

Obviously, you will need to have researched more than just your service line and you will need to speak coherently about this and other firms' offerings, in general.

Which qualification have you chosen and why? What is involved in this?

You need to know why you are going for CIMA, ACCA, ACA or CIPFA – the earlier chapters should help, but you should also have scrutinised the professional bodies' websites.

Think about your performance afterwards – what could you have answered better or differently? Before you come off the telephone, make sure that you have a contact name, whom you might subsequently call for feedback.

First interview

Hopefully you have got through to the first interview stage! The first interview is likely to last about 45 minutes to one hour and is generally face to face, although telephone and virtual interviews can often be arranged. The interviewer (usually a senior manager from your chosen service, or possibly HR) simply wants to know that you want to, and can, do the job and that you will fit in. At this stage, interviewers will therefore be primarily exploring your motivation – why you want to join the firm and what your understanding is about the nature of the work (do you *really* want to do it and know what you are in for?), and getting a feel for you as a person.

The interview is likely to focus on your application form and previous experiences, and questions will be standardised (every candidate will be asked the same things to ensure fairness). The key competencies they will be looking for are likely to be:

- commercial awareness and focus

- relationship building and teamwork

- leadership, motivation skills

- problem solving and analysis

- drive and resilience

- ambition and career-mindedness

- influencing skills and initiative

- organisational skills.

Additionally, they will be assessing you on:

- image, professionalism, respectability and responsibility

- ethics, integrity, trustworthiness and truthfulness.

Commercial awareness

This perhaps warrants a special look, because this is a nebulous concept, but one much bandied around. If you have read business and finance at university, this competency may be taken as 'ticked', but what of humanities, arts, science, engineering and social science graduates?

Everyone has to undertake work experience in year 10 at school, and hopefully you will also have undertaken vacation work and maybe some paid work during a gap year. Think about the firm you worked for: what did you learn about that company; did they meet the needs of the customer; how did they market themselves; what would you have done differently; how could they have developed?

Perhaps you were an active member of a student society or of rag week? How did you market events, and attract new members or fundraisers? Did you have to budget, assess costs or act as treasurer?

Keep up to date with current affairs and business news; read the broadsheets and *Financial Times*, especially anything pertinent to accountancy and to the firm to which you are applying. The *Financial Times* is an obvious daily read, but if short on time, you should register for its daily email feed summarising the news of the day.

Preparation

- Remind yourself of desired skills and competencies and list several examples of situations and behaviours that demonstrate these.

- Think about possible questions and practise responses.

- Plan your (conservative) attire, route and travel timings (a practice run can be a good idea if not too far away – you might then also take this opportunity to stand outside and see what people are wearing), and a checklist of things to take with you (perhaps a clipboard with a copy of your application form and CV, names of interviewers, map and contact details of the firm, company literature, details of referees, diary, notes and pen).

- Prepare some good questions which you might ask them.

On the day

The interviewer remembers the beginning and end of the session, so you need to start and finish well. Usually, the opposite occurs because nerves spoil interviewees' performances at first and tiredness contributes to flagging at the end.

- Arrive early so that you might relax and compose yourself.

- Turn off your mobile.

- Think about body language: confident entry, firm handshake, smile, eye contact, face as many interviewers as possible – turn the chair if necessary to sit at 45 degrees, yet still able to see the whole panel (less like facing a firing squad!). Do not slouch or shuffle; cross your legs at the ankle and relax and breathe normally.

- Take cues from the interviewers' body language as well: nodding shows encouragement, leaning forward shows interest, whereas folded arms and finger drumming can be less positive signs!

- The interviewer will make all manner of assumptions about your socio-economic, intellectual, educational, religious, political, and sexual persuasions in the first few seconds, so look and act the part!

- Listen and do not interrupt.

- Be truthful and positive (not gushing).

- Do not ramble or gabble, be specific, vary your tone of voice, and avoid clichés and 'um's and 'er's.

Typical questions, prompts and probes

Practise the following questions and you should be able to handle most questions thrown at you.

- What have you found out about our business?

- Why have you decided to apply to us, in particular?

- What has been your biggest challenge to date?

- How are you able to juggle your commitments?

- Give me two examples of when you worked in a team. What was your role?

- Describe a time when you were in a conflict situation. How did you handle it? Explain how you chose to do the correct thing. What was the outcome?

- Tell me about a situation where you have successfully persuaded someone to change their point of view. What was the situation? How did you manage to persuade them? What was the result?

- Your tasks are feeling routine: how do you keep yourself motivated?

- Describe a current issue in the business world.

- Which company do you believe has potential for growth, and why?

- Provide an example of a company which has grown a lot in the last couple of years. What would you advise them to do next?

- In your opinion, what problems are professional services firms currently facing?

- What are your strengths?

- What are your development needs?

- How would your team describe you?

- Describe a complex problem you had to deal with recently. What was the problem? How did you resolve it? How did you ensure that you understood all facts and had considered all alternative solutions?

- How did you structure your time at university, to ensure that you balanced your personal life?

- Why professional services/industry/public sector?

- Where do you see yourself in five years' time? What are your long-term career objectives?

- What would you say have been your major achievements to date?

- What is the role of a graduate here?

- Tell us about the biggest mistake you have made. What did you learn from your experience?

- Have you applied for any other graduate jobs?

- How does this organisation add value to its clients?

- How is assurance divided and in which division would you like to work?

- Tell me what you know about the qualification which you will be studying?

- Detail a situation when you were working towards a deadline and the parameters were changed. What did you do?

- Which recent developments have strongly affected the accounting industry?

- What can you tell me about the line of service to which you have applied?

- Discuss a recent piece of financial news which has been in the press.

- Give an example of a time when you have had to take corrective action and change your plans. Why was this necessary? What did you do? What was the outcome?

- Describe a time when you had to gather large amounts of data. How did you gather it? What systems did you use?

- When have you identified an error due to strong attention to detail? How did you identify the problem? What was the result?

Questions you might ask

One way to leave a positive impression is to have some really good questions prepared. Now is the time to get your own back! Ask about yourself, the particular role and about the organisation.

- Now you have met me, what reservations do you have? What would be the greatest challenges for me?

- How and when will my performance be appraised?

- This is a structured organisation; what opportunity is there for meritocratic progress? When might I expect to be promoted? When is the earliest anyone has been promoted?

- What scope is there for independence and initiative?

- What percentage of trainees are lost in the first year? First three years?

- What is the policy on examination failures (you do not want to look as if you lack confidence, but you do need to know)?

- How would you describe the cultural climate of this firm?

- Where do you see the company going in the next few years? What challenges does it face? Is any restructuring planned?

- Why do you believe I should join this firm rather than a competitor?

- When might I expect to hear and to start (if this has not already been discussed)?

- You mentioned xyz earlier – would you tell me more about that please?

Assessment centre

This is the last stage in the recruitment and selection process. It often comprises further psychometric tests and interviews, e-tray and group exercises, and perhaps a presentation.

Preparation

Take heart in the fact that you have made it thus far, so the first interviewer liked you enough to put you forward and you must be doing something right.

- All materials for the assessments should be provided, but you may be allowed to use your own calculator if you are more comfortable and familiar with this.

- Check that you have any necessary spectacles, hearing aids and medication.

- Notify them of any disabilities or special needs.

Psychometric measures

The firm may have sent some practice psychometric tests, but see tips above as well.

Second interview

The interview tips given on p221 are equally relevant at this stage – keep in mind the competencies being assessed throughout the day.

Group exercises

- In group exercises, speak clearly and audibly to ensure that you are heard (by candidates and assessors).

- Offer to be scribe so that you take control, gaining attention and becoming pivotal in summarising, decision-making and recording of action plans.

- Make sure that you repeat the comments of others to demonstrate that you are listening and then expand and give your own opinion, and suggest compromises where relevant.

- Let others have their say. Ask for votes or group consensus, and make decisions where this cannot be reached.

- Clearly state what has been proposed and plan action, agreeing who will be responsible for what and by when.

- Do not make enemies: fellow candidates may well soon be your colleagues. Remember that in large firms, you are not in competition with them, but all seeking selection individually.

- Monitor the time.

E-tray exercise (electronic equivalent of an in-tray exercise)

These look at your approach and ability to manage a sample of tasks similar to those required in the actual job. Usually, you will have a scenario described and will need to appropriately handle emails and requests from various parties and stakeholders as they enter your inbox. This will involve prioritisation, decision-making, sensitive handling of information and people (who may be demanding or disgruntled), organisation, information research, collation and assimilation, and data analysis. A given booklet will set the scene and explain the situation, and the roles of various parties. Emails may speed up as the time runs out, putting on pressure, and requiring good time management and prioritisation. Answers are multiple choice.

Tips

- Do not rush, because some questions are devised to mislead and it is easy to jump to conclusions.

- Be diplomatic and upset no one.

- Try a practice e-tray exercise like the one on the Civil Service website: http://faststream.civilservice.gov.uk/How-do-I-apply/Example-e-Tray-Excercise [sic.]

- Read instructions and information carefully to fully familiarise yourself with the situation. Be prepared to shelve emails which you cannot answer due to lack of information, or to make judgement calls where appropriate. Sometimes sitting on the email allows time for the missing bit of the jigsaw to fit into place.

- It is important to check whether you can change an answer, reopen an email which you have temporarily shelved, or even alter a reply which you have closed or sent.

- Double check your calculations, because the most common wrong answers are often included!

Written exercise

This will generally involve reading company data and information, comparing and making choices and recommendations regarding strategy. You need to be able to defend your choices and arguments.

Tips

- Your writing will need to be grammatical and audience-specific, and ideally without spelling mistakes.

- Manage your time so that you give equal attention to each company or section.

- Communication skills and logical analysis will be assessed in the way that you construct the report and argue your points.

Lunch

Remember, you could still be being watched and assessed over lunch, and assessors may want to see how you might interact and build relationships with clients, so ensure that you are friendly, charming and polite. Again, fellow candidates could soon be your peers!

Presentation

You may be required to give a short presentation. This could be part of a group exercise (in which case you must work together as a cohesive team), or you may be briefed individually ahead of time. Stick to time limits. Argue points clearly and concisely and be prepared to defend your claims and recommendations. You are not being assessed on your fancy IT skills, but on your ability to assimilate and understand information and to communicate clearly, logically and persuasively.

After

You should hear within a few days. If unsuccessful, try not to be despondent; congratulate yourself on having made it so far, ask for feedback and aim to learn from the experience.

Case study

Nicola Day is a Senior Associate in Assurance at PwC.

I started at PwC in April 2009 after completing a summer internship in 2007. The selection process for the internship was exactly the same as for the graduate scheme and so following the placement, I was offered a full time role to begin when I finished university.

The first stage of the process was to complete an online application form and an online numerical reasoning test. The application form covered areas such as my academic qualifications and expected university grade, my reasons for applying for the role and other areas such as my outside interests and hobbies. The test was done online and was timed, with a series of short maths-based multiple choice questions to answer. A good background in GCSE maths would have been good enough to pass it.

After getting through the applications stage and test, I was invited to my chosen PwC office in Newcastle. Here, I took two further tests and took part in a group discussion. We were presented with some brief information beforehand and given time to prepare specific points to discuss. There were four people in the group and the assessors observed us putting forward our points and listening to others.

After the group assessment, I was interviewed by a manager in my chosen department, assurance. During the interview I was mainly asked why I wanted to work for PwC and what I thought the job would entail. I was also asked about any recent business issue that had caught my attention. Finally, I was asked to describe situations where I had demonstrated initiative and teamwork in the past. Although formal, the interview was relaxed and was a chance for me to get to know more about PwC.

At the end of the assessment day, we were invited to lunch with some current graduate trainees to wind down and ask any further questions that we had.

I was invited back to meet a director at the firm. He asked me a series of business-based questions which relied upon common sense rather than any prior business knowledge. For example, I remember one question being: 'You are a large supermarket chain in the north-east and you are looking to open some new stores. What would you consider in making this decision?' He was looking for sensible suggestions and gave me plenty of time to think about my answers.

To prepare for the application process, I attended some PwC events at university and researched their website so that I had a good idea of what they did and who they were.

My advice would be to play to your strengths and be yourself. The group exercise is an opportunity to show that you can come up with sensible ideas but also that you can listen well to others. When it comes to the interview stage, I never felt like they were trying to 'catch me out'. They want to see people with confidence and enthusiasm who have a well-rounded life outside of academia, as ultimately they will be putting you in front of their clients from an early stage.

8

Support through training

It can seem a long and lonely road when you are poring over accountancy books and study materials, especially after a hard day's work. It takes a lot of self-discipline and intellectual rigour, and it can help for you to have someone to talk to for both morale and practical support. Obviously, you need to be seen to be putting in the effort as well: do not request holidays early on, in busy periods, or when examinations are looming; do not skip any classes or mock examinations; put in the necessary study hours and revision; plan your study timetable and stick to it – do not let friends and family talk you into partying when you should have your nose to the grindstone!

With the larger firms, there are likely to be other trainees with whom to compare notes and provide mutual support, commiserations and/or congratulations, but in smaller set-ups and internal roles, you could be the only one going through it at that particular time. So to whom might you turn for support?

Your employing company

On official training schemes, the company is expected (and perhaps contracted) to provide you with study leave, support with fees, and relevant and varied experience at the right time. Larger firms may have hundreds of trainees at the same time, and are well set up to give you training, development and coaching sessions, and structured support, and are committed to ensuring that you realise your true potential and achieve your goals. The selection, training and development of staff is costly, so they want to minimalise failure and attrition for both the individual's and the company's sake.

Whether Public Practices or companies, employers will start with capable people who have strong problem-solving ability and commercial focus. They will value integrity and the talent to work well in a team and to build positive working relationships. They will appreciate the ability to learn from experience, even mistakes, and to bring out the best in others, but they will also aim to build on such innate potential and softer people skills, through nurturing talent and ensuring that trainees acquire solid technical skills and develop both personally and professionally.

KPMG, for example, planned to take on in excess of 1,000 graduates, school leavers and interns in 2010, and claims to be the only firm with a dedicated full-time professional qualification training (PQT) team. Their pass rates speak for themselves!

- **They spread training over the three years, so that you will not be studying continuously, and by the final, most technical papers, you will have 2 and a half years' practical experience to boost your understanding and maximise your chances of passing first time.**

- **They vary the type of training to include classroom and practical elements, and online packages through which you might progress at a pace to suit yourself.**

- **KPMG allow deferrals of examinations for people who feel insufficiently prepared, so that they do not place trainees under unnecessary stress and lower confidence through failures.**

- **They have a strong diversity team to ensure that the necessary support is provided in cases of disability, illness, religious observance, and so on.**

Nestlé, on the other hand, offers graduates financial support and generous study leave (five days per examination) towards CIMA qualification. You may prefer to take day release to attend college during the day, or you may want to go to college in the evening, or, then again, you may choose to spend weekends at college and keep study leave for revision days before the examination.

Your boss

Obviously, your boss was once a trainee and, while no doubt busy themselves, should be willing to help, advise and support you. Don't be too proud to admit that you are finding something difficult and to ask for an explanation of a topic – look at the pass rates for accountancy qualifications: not everyone is able to pass first time! Pick your time carefully (not when against the clock with an imminent end of month or year return), and request a quiet meeting – better to own up than completely mess up! You should be having regular sessions with your direct line manager for setting targets and giving feedback on performance and progress, in any event. Ask to be given relevant, stretching and varied hands-on experience to help consolidate your learning.

Your personal career coach

Many firms will assign you a personal development mentor or coach; someone committed to your career development rather than your line manager who is more interested in your standard of work. This person advises and supports as you progress through the organisation. Sometimes, you will additionally be allotted a peer 'buddy' for the induction stage.

Course tutors with training organisations

It harms training providers' reputations should you fail to pass your examinations; they often market themselves on their students' success rates, so training providers should also be happy to help and advise if you feel that you do not understand and are struggling with a certain paper or topic. They will usually allot a personal tutor, and they also run strategically timed revision programmes.

Professional bodies' student support services

The professional bodies will vary in what they can offer you in terms of support throughout your training. Below we've given you a few examples of the kind of support on offer. It's a really good idea to do some research into this, and make the most of the resources available to you.

ICAEW/ACA

The below list from the ICAEW website identifies the ways in which professional bodies might support and advise.

The ICAEW/ACA have a full-time, dedicated student support team to assist with:

- initial registrations

- training contract matters

- initial professional development (IPD) and work based learning

- friendly reminders of key dates and exam entry deadlines

- access to our award-winning business library and information service

- access to your local student network group via the student district societies

- examination-related enquiries

- change of address

- requests for literature

- overseas enquiries

- student discounts and offers

- up-to-date practice case studies.

Source: www.icaew.com; studentsupport@icaew.com

CIMA

CIMA has a student discussion forum and blog for students to network and post their queries. It produces a starter pack, has a dedicated students area on its website and publishes both student and professional member magazines. Go to www. cimaglobal.com/Employers/CIMA-Training/Student-support to find out more.

ACCA

ACCA emphasises its global reach for tuition, examination, employment and support:

- 83 offices and centres worldwide offering you support while you study

- 646 tuition providers worldwide

- over 380 exam centres in 170 countries so you can sit your exams locally

- 8,424 approved employers offering you quality study and training support.

Furthermore, the firm organises events, careers fairs and webinars during which one might network or quiz examiners:

- webcasts where you can question examiners

- exam technique events

- careers fairs

- discussions on key topics affecting the profession.

See the website www.accaglobal.com/en/qualifications/why-acca/support for further details.

CIPFA

CIPFA runs a student helpline for problems while working through the open learning materials and support on:

- exemptions

- examination and case study preparation

- examination deadlines and registration

- help with the Study Lounge

- Initial Professional Development Scheme (IPDS).

You can email studentsupport@cipfa.org.uk for more information.

Financial support

For ACA training, and when you are employed on a Training Contract, the employer will generally fund the cost of training and examinations (at least, the first attempt). Some training bodies will offer reductions for people paying their own fees. Obviously, you would be working and earning, but there may be opportunities for help with costs from grant-providing bodies, or through career development loans. See both www.turn2us.org.uk and www.direct.gov.uk/en/EducationAndLearning/ AdultLearning/FinancialHelpForAdultLearners/CareerDevelopmentLoans.

As a registered student, you will be eligible for an NUS student discount card, which can provide eligibility for travel, leisure, driving lessons and consumer products. Publishers will often offer reductions on books and even the *Financial Times*. See www.nus.org.uk/en/NUS-Extra/Discounts.

Relationships

Do not forget that relationships can suffer when one is too busy with work and study to give others the attention they need or desire. You may be feeling sorry for yourself, but others may be feeling neglected and pushed out, too.

It is important to create some balance in your life and to make sure that you have fun and do not let it be 'all work and no play'. You need to rest, recuperate and laugh for your physical and mental well-being.

Speak to your partner if you are irritable or stressed, explaining how you are feeling and apologising for your tiredness or poor humour. Not only may they be pacified, but you may feel unburdened as well. Ask them to lighten the load by helping with more domestic chores when you are revising, and by allowing you space to think and study. Perhaps you could even include them by inviting them to test you?

Counsellors

Examinations can be very stressful, especially when your whole career seems to hinge on the outcome. Fear of failure can be cumulative, as you have to consistently live up to previous achievements. Instead of looking at the evidence and thinking: 'Well, I did well before, why should I not do well again?', people can start to feel like a fraud and believe that it was a fluke that they were successful before, that it was only because they worked so hard, and they won't be able to do it again.

Strategies for avoiding study might then begin to emerge, and procrastination, obsessing and negative thinking. This needs to be nipped in the bud, and some cognitive behaviour therapy with a counsellor can give you valuable coping techniques and enable you to adjust how you talk to yourself and behave. Many larger firms provide private health insurance and employee benefit allowances, which could fund this.

Try to remember that you have already been designated bright enough through the psychometric assessments during selection – you clearly do have the ability, and if the other 424,000 qualified accountants in the world could pass their examination, so too can you!

9

Qualified: what next?

Post-qualification

Once qualified in accountancy, the career opportunities really open up. One of the joys of accountancy is that there are endless career possibilities, depending on how your interests, personality, skills and experience develop. You can move to different companies, roles, sectors and practice specialisms. As the common career paths table in chapter 3 showed, there is a great deal of potential movement, both upwards and sideways.

During the first few years, you will progress and develop through gaining experience and taking on greater responsibility, whether supervising and leading others, working on more technically complex issues, or on higher-visibility, bigger-value projects for more important clients.

Public Practice

In Public Practice, the structure tends to be quite formal, and you become increasingly responsible for managing risk and bringing in the business; relationship building is an increasingly important element of more senior roles. You will manage client relationships and identify opportunities for growing and developing the practice. You will also lead people initiatives.

In audit, you would develop broad business knowledge and increasing technical competence in accounting, tax, accounting and IT processes, financial reporting and so on. In tax, you would take responsibility for more complex projects, maintaining quality while adhering to compliance standards. Advisory services include risk, mergers and acquisitions, corporate finance, business and financial management, and performance improvement offerings, and you would be managing multiple projects of increasing complexity. Of course, post-qualification, you are no longer tied to that employer and you may decide to move to a larger or smaller practice where there are different types or challenges and opportunities.

You could expect to be in a senior role within two to three years, working through senior management and reaching executive director within nine to 12 years and achieving senior executive partner in 10 to 15 years.

Secondments

Also in Public Practice, you might, post-qualification, transfer to a different professional specialism, such as tax, consultancy, forensic accountancy, risk, insolvency or corporate finance. Be aware that movement from tax in the opposite direction can be more difficult, because you may be viewed as too specialised, especially if you have studied tax rather than accountancy qualifications. Transfer between practice specialisms is easier at junior level, before you are seen as too specialised.

You might be seconded to an internal role on a client's site, or perhaps abroad to a different office. Secondments can be a good way not only of gaining experience but also of trying out different fields without being committed. Most people planning an external move do so within three years of qualification.

Of course, secondments abroad can sometimes be surprisingly different and not the 'jolly in the sun' you expect! You are there to do a job and it has been said that a surprising number of accountants seconded to the Australian office ask to return home early; the very high proportion of Asian colleagues means that the culture may be very serious and 'eyes down, no talking' – quite different from the more relaxed and friendly London ethos.

Mobility and working overseas

Secondments are equally an option if you are working internally for a global firm, and ACCA- and CIMA-qualified accountants may also relocate both in the UK and abroad, within or between companies, on a permanent or temporary basis.

When planning your career and selecting firms to apply to, it is obviously sensible to factor travel into the equation. (Do also ask about the opportunities at interview, because you cannot just assume that moving abroad will be an option.) In all fields of accountancy, if you are prepared to be mobile and to relocate within and between firms, your promotion prospects and career progression will be aided.

Internal moves

Your typical first positions, when moving from Public Practice into an in-house role as an ACA-qualified accountant, would be internal auditor, financial accountant, or perhaps roles in governance or business analysis (quite objective and technical roles). CIMA-qualified accountants, on the other hand, have a broader commercial training and could move into more senior financial roles, into different sectors (such as banking, venture capital, manufacturing, retail, FMCG, or perhaps public sector), or even into different functions (perhaps supply chain, marketing and strategy fields), or different careers (for instance, management consultancy). Similarly, the wide business and financial syllabus and strategic emphasis of ACCA means that if you are ACCA-qualified, you can also move into broader business management and consultancy.

With a CIPFA qualification, you might move in the opposite direction, into Public Practice, or you might move upwards internally or to different governmental and not-for-profit concerns. Mobility will be important for progression, and career paths in financial management tend to be structured, yet with opportunities to develop and specialise. Challenging and rewarding opportunities may be found in the NHS, local and central government; within several years of qualification, you may be taking responsibility for considerable resources or entire departments.

Most firms have qualified accountants in senior roles, whether as financial or operational directors or as CEOs (20% of CEOs in the FTSE 100 are qualified accountants).

Self-employment

There is always the option of starting your own accountancy practice with a relevant practising certificate, or, indeed, your own business. As an accountant, you will of course have a very good understanding of how to make a business successful and the internal controls required to cope with cashflow issues in early days.

Management consultancy

Management consultancy is another future career move which you might consider, whether starting your own consultancy in the longer term, or joining an established organisation. The Big Four audit firms have their own consulting divisions which provide services to manage talent, reduce costs and risk, improve quality, customer service, efficiency and performance, ensure smooth transactions in mergers and acquisitions, and advise on strategic direction. As a qualified accountant you could have a lot to contribute due to your technical, financial and business knowledge and experience, and while it is also possible to start as a new graduate, it is also common for experienced professionals to transfer to the consultancy division of that or a competitor firm, or into a smaller consultancy.

Continuing professional development (CPD)

Professional bodies recognise that qualification is the beginning, not the end for professional development, and you would be required to keep up to date and professionally competent throughout your career.

ACA

Initial personal development (IPD) is part of the ACA qualifying process and is required to integrate experience with academic studies and learned skills, through considering and recording issues relating to:

- ethics and professionalism

- personal effectiveness

- technical and functional expertise

- business awareness

- professional judgement.

Beyond qualification, continuing professional development (CPD) ensures ongoing currency and competence and maintains the reputation, credibility and value of ACA accreditation. This may include building on communication and management skills, ethical awareness, business awareness and legal and regulatory knowledge. The ICAEW encourages reflection to:

- identify gaps in your knowledge, skills and competencies, perhaps as a result of changes in your environment, role, responsibilities or the world

- consider risks inherent in your role and the expectations of others on you – your weaknesses personally and technically

- undertake appropriate learning and development activities to help you address these needs

- assess the effectiveness of these activities and consider whether your learning and development objectives have been met.

There is a great deal of freedom and flexibility. Development may be self-directed and through any medium to suit your lifestyle and personal needs, and there are no set number of hours or points to attain. You might attend courses, conferences, workshops or seminars, take additional courses (electronic or classroom-based), or undertake personal reading, perhaps in professional magazines and technical journals. The only requirement is that you keep an online CPD record, so that you can produce evidence of continued professional development, should it ever be requested.

CIMA

CIMA also recognises that, in part through globalisation, financial management functions and regulations undergo constant change. In line with the IFAC

(International Federation of Accountants) standard practice, CPD is required, but is flexible and it is considered your own responsibility to identify and address the needs for both professional and career development. A strong ethical code and integrity is not enough alone; you need hard skills like project management, communication and teamwork as well.

CIMA's scheme emphasises the output rather than the number of hours or units of formal learning. The organisation feels this addresses its busy members' diverse working environments best. But you are invited to regular training workshops and networking events. CIMA recognises over 100 employers as accredited partners providing relevant CPD, and has developed a range of supporting CPD resources, valued planning tools and materials. Members are reported as saying CPD activities have yielded positive results and do indeed further their careers. With three years' strategic experience, you can apply for CIMA Fellowship (FCMA), which adds further weight to a CV.

CIPFA

CPD is mandatory for CIPFA members, too, and as with CIMA, many public sector bodies operate accredited staff development programmes. Career progression requires learning through meetings, conferences and training courses.

The CIPFA Learning Centre enables members to manage their CPD online and access authoritative learning materials. Your minimum requirement is 20 hours in one year and 120 hours over three years. CPD does not have to be at a cost; it is anything that enhances your skills and knowledge relevant to the job – even, for instance, volunteering your services to a community group or a CIPFA panel or working group. By recording and planning your CPD, you should be better able to identify areas of expertise or development needs for career progression.

ACCA

ACCA additionally emphasises that professionalism is about lifelong learning in order to meet the needs of a changing market. Again, you are afforded flexibility and control over how much and what development activities you choose to undertake. However, ACCA has introduced the 'Realise' professional development programme to help plan, manage and record progress in building learning and skills, alongside codes of ethics and professionalism. This scheme provides clear reassurance that you are keeping yourself up to date. ACCA requires that you submit an annual CPD declaration.

ACCA recognises certain approved employers which provide excellent development and training, and lists accredited CPD training providers (face to face courses, and technical updates, qualifications and presentations). The organisation also provides a virtual learning centre with a wide range of courses and materials for Public Practice.

The future of accountancy

Moving with the times

As new blood enters the accounting profession, we are seeing more online accounting systems being established, with reports of online accounting vendors being mobbed for demonstrations at conferences! Moving with the times, the power of social media is also being embraced by some in the accounting world, as Twitter and LinkedIn become the preferred channels to generate business and engage with clients.

Sustainability and ethics

"Wise are those who learn that the bottom line doesn't always have to be their top priority."

William Arthur Ward

Corporate social responsibility is increasingly recognised as important in today's world, both to attract clients, investors and potential employees, and to maintain a positive, ethical, honourable and altruistic image with stakeholders and the wider community.

Professional bodies and accountancy firms are not only concerned about integrity regarding legal and governance issues, but also about people and environmental concerns; they increasingly want to be seen to be keen to 'give something back' and to actively reduce their carbon footprint. Accountancy professions clearly need to be just as vigilant and enlightened in advising clients, as in working within their own employing companies – the stereotypical, 'black or white' accountant could more naturally concentrate on the bottom line, and perhaps neglect to invest in more nebulous image factors or to incorporate CSR initiatives into strategy. Sweatshops may reduce costs but will be bad for business; fair trade and 'environmentally friendly' sells! Sponsorship and donation of funds raise a company's profile and image. Good pay, perks, and training and development attract and keep quality employees. Sustainability is important not just ethically but commercially.

At least one ICAEW member is included in 85% of FTSE company boards, so accountants are ideally placed to impact on a firm's ethical performance, in addition to its commercial efficiency. Ethical components are increasingly included, and indeed weighted heavily, in accountancy training and professional development. CIMA and DEFRA have actively collaborated to design a 'Climate Resilience Tool'; the ICAEW have launched an e-learning Business Sustainability Programme; and ethics, social, and environmental issues are at the heart of the ACCA qualification. (One compulsory business analysis paper requires students to examine the impact of social and environmental factors on the strategy of a business, and the scope of CSR in relation to the expectations of stakeholders.)

The Prince of Wales is keen for sustainability in accountancy to become part of the DNA of businesses today and tomorrow. The Accounting for Sustainability project (www.accountingforsustainability.org) is working with multi-disciplinary agencies, like public, not-for-profit and commercial sector organisations, professional bodies, investors, and academics to develop key guidelines and tools to ensure sustainability is fundamental to reporting and decision-making.

"The buck stops with the guy who signs the cheques."

Rupert Murdoch

Globalisation

Accountancy bodies listen to their members and tailor learning and support to address these members' needs. At the same time as incorporating sustainability and ethics into their curriculums, they are also considering globalisation. Growing globalisation is increasingly not just about career mobility, but also the need for standardised international practices and greater concern for, and focus on, sustainability factors. By about 2012, the UK GAAP accounting standards should be superseded by International Financial Reporting Standards (IFRS). As the global downturn demonstrated, we are inextricably linked and intertwined.

Globalisation has also increased competition and greater outsourcing of business processes and shared services. Outsourced functions may not only be in a different part of the country, but even a different part of the world! Cheaper and more advanced telecommunications are having an ever-increasing impact on businesses. Accountants need to recognise and run with such changes. Of course, technological advances may also free up finance professionals from more mundane and routine accounting, and give them more time for involvement in strategic and commercial decision-making.

"For a lot of people, the weekly paycheck is 'take-home pay' because home is the only place they can afford to go with it."

Charles A Jaffe

Conclusion

Accountancy has always been a sought-after qualification and a ticket to a successful career, whether in professional practice or as a springboard into a senior commercial or a managerial role. The profession's future is rosy, and now is a great time to start your career in accountancy.

Increasingly, in this competitive market, qualifications count, and employers seem to demand ever higher grades, more prestigious qualifications, and directly relevant experience. However, firms are also introducing appealing school leaver schemes to attract strong candidates earlier, and with the raising of university fees, it may be that fewer people go for graduate entry and select school-leaver and the AAT or CAT routes instead.

There is said to be a global shortage of finance-qualified professionals, and companies are increasingly turning to accountants to help them weather the current economic storm. Those prepared to take a tough stance on risk, costs and waste (including changes to executive rewards and bonus schemes!) are being welcomed.

A high demand for qualified accountants is being predicted, often for opposing reasons. When times are bad, accountants are needed to manage the negative situation, and when things are improving, more accountants will be needed to meet the demand due to the economic growth and to manage the increasingly complex accounting and reporting procedures. Whichever is the case, sound judgement and communication will be required, with fluency in current affairs to complement technical excellence – and accountancy remains the universal language of business.

There are so many routes into accountancy that suit a variety of personalities and situations. We hope that in this book, you've found the information and tools you need to decide what's right for you, and take your first steps into your long and successful accounting career.

Useful resources

Professional accountancy bodies

- **Institute of Chartered Accountants in England & Wales (ICAEW):** www.icaew.com

- **Institute of Chartered Accountants of Scotland:** www.icas.org.uk

- **Institute of Chartered Accountants of Ireland:** www.icai.ie

- **Association of Chartered Certified Accountants (ACCA):** www.acca.co.uk

- **Chartered Institute of Management Accountants (CIMA):** www.cimaglobal.com

- **Chartered Institute of Public Finance and Accountancy (CIPFA):** www.cipfa.org.uk

- **National Audit Office:** www.nao.org.uk

- **NHS Financial Management Training Scheme:** www.futureleaders.nhs.uk

- **London Treasurers Local Government Finance Graduate Scheme:** www.financethefuture.com

- **Institute of Financial Accountants (IFA):** www.ifa.org.uk

- **Chartered Institute of Taxation:** www.tax.org.uk

- **Association of International Associates (AIA):** www.aiaworldwide.com

- **Association of Corporate Treasurers (ACT):** www.treasurers.org

- **Association of Accounting Technicians (AAT):** www.aat.org.uk

Accountancy qualifications

A list of accredited training providers for each professional body may be found on the tuition provider pages of professional body websites and also at www. accountancystudents.co.uk/resources/tuition_providers.

Financial support

- **Turn 2 Us Financial Support:** www.turn2us.org.uk

- **Career Development Loans:** www.direct.gov.uk/en/ EducationAndLearning/AdultLearning/FinancialHelpForAdultLearners/ CareerDevelopmentLoans

- **National Union of Students:** www.nus.org.uk/en/NUS-Extra/ Discounts

Support for school leavers

- **Kaplan Financial:** http://financial.kaplan.co.uk and http:// kaplanapprenticeships.co.uk

- **The Apprenticeship Scheme:** www.apprenticeships.org.uk

- **Learning and Skills Council Train to Gain Scheme:** www.traintogain. gov.uk

- **Funding in Scotland:** www.skillsdevelopmentscotland.co.uk

- **Funding in Wales:** www.new.wales.gov.uk

- **Funding in Northern Ireland:** www.delni.gov.uk

Vacancy information

Internships

- www.internoptions.com

- www.targetjobs.co.uk

- www.allaboutcareers.com

- www.milkround.com

- www.ratemyplacement.co.uk

Trainee vacancies may be found on the websites of the professional bodies. See also:

- **Accountancy Age Jobs:** www.accountancyagejobs.com

- **Accountant Careers:** www.accountantcareers.co.uk

- **Association of Chartered Certified Accountants:** www.accaglobal.com

- **Joslin Rowe:** www.joslinrowe.com

- **Audit Jobs & Careers:** www.careersinaudit.com

- **Local Government Jobs:** www.lgjobs.com

- **TaxWorking:** www.taxworking.org

- **Swatuk:** www.swat.co.uk

Interview preparation

- **Psychometric tests:** www.jobtestprep.co.uk

- **Assessment Day:** www.assessmentday.co.uk

General accountancy information

- **Accounting web:** www.accountingweb.co.uk

- **Public Finance:** www.publicfinance.co.uk

- **PQ Accountant magazine:** www.pqaccountant.com

Accounting and the environment

- **The Accounting for Sustainability Project:** www. accountingforsustainability.org

General careers information

- **Accountancy Students:** www.accountancystudents.co.uk

- **Allaboutcareers:** www.allaboutcareers.com

- **Prospects:** www.prospects.ac.uk

- **Inside Careers:** www.insidecareers.co.uk

- **UCAS:** www.ucas.com

Index of advertisers

Working in Accountancy